How to Win the Trust of a Scorpio

Real Life Guidance on How to get Along
and Be Friends with the Eighth Sign
of the Zodiac

How to Win the Trust of a Scorpio

Real Life Guidance on How to get Along and Be Friends with the Eighth Sign of the Zodiac

Mary English

Winchester, UK
Washington, USA

First published by Dodona Books, 2012
Dodona Books is an imprint of John Hunt Publishing Ltd., Laurel House, Station Approach,
Alresford, Hants, SO24 9JH, UK
office1@jhpbooks.net
www.johnhuntpublishing.com
www.dodona-books.com

For distributor details and how to order please visit the 'Ordering' section on our website.

Text copyright: Mary English 2011

ISBN: 978 1 78099 351 5

A CIP catalogue record for this book is available from the British Library.

Design: Lee Nash

Printed and bound by CPI Group (UK) Ltd, Croydon, CR0 4YY

We operate a distinctive and ethical publishing philosophy in all
areas of our business, from our global network of authors to
production and worldwide distribution.

CONTENTS

This book is dedicated to S.K.
Still Waters Run Deep

Acknowledgements

I would like to thank the following people:
My son for being the Libran that always makes me look on the other side.
My Taurus husband Jonathan for being the most wonderful man in my world.
Mabel, Jessica and Usha for their Homeopathic help and understanding.
Laura and Mandy for their friendship.
Donna Cunningham for her help and advice.
Judy Hall for her inspiration.
Alois Treindl for being the Pisces that founded the wonderful Astro.com website
Judy Ramsell Howard at the Bach Centre for her encouragement.
John my publisher for being the person that fought tooth and nail to get this book published and all the staff at O-Books including Lee, Trevor, Kate, Catherine, Maria and Mary.
Oksana, Mary S, Cherry, Polly, Renee, Elaine and Miriam for their welcome editing eyes.
And last but not least my lovely clients for their valued contributions.

Introduction

In almost every profession — whether it's law or journalism, finance or medicine or academia or running a small business — people rely on confidential communications to do their jobs. We count on the space of trust that confidentiality provides. When someone breaches that trust, we are all worse off for it.
Hillary Clinton

Why the title of this book? My first book *How to Survive a Pisces* was written to help people understand the sign that I am: Pisces. When the book was accepted for publication, I was told that this was only on the understanding that I didn't just write one book. More spookily the publisher himself is also a Pisces, so it sort of made sense that he might accept my book for publication...I only found this out afterwards but it set me thinking that maybe life isn't just a random event.

When I'd finished the first book clients and friends (and family) asked me when was I going to write about *their* sign...and this series of books was born.

I work as an Astrologer 'on the front line' and I have firsthand knowledge of the worries and upsetments that clients come to me with, and this book is written from that perspective. It's not written for those that are having a wonderful life, full or roses, happy faces and contentment.

No, it's written to help those people struggling with Life the Universe and Everything (as fellow Pisces Douglas Adams said) and especially with the 8th sign of the Zodiac: Scorpio.

You might be a Scorpio yourself, or your child/partner or relative or friend is one. You might want to learn a little about Astrology, which I shall explain, or more importantly a little about how a Scorpio thinks and lives their life.

As each book is written with examples from 'real life' it was funny when I posted onto my Facebook page: 'are there any Scorpios who want to share their thoughts with me?' and after a few hours I was getting messages in my inbox (as opposed to on my wall where I had written this)

Personal private messages.

How Scorpio that was!

Now if I'd asked that same question of Leos, my wall would have been flooded with funny, tragic, dramatic 'look at me' comments...

No, the Scorpios replied but the messages were one-to-one, not visible to anyone else and sent to my messages or my private email address.

I also asked the same question on air on Talk Radio Europe where I have spot with Hannah Murray and the same thing happened.

Personal messages, one-to-one and enquiring exactly what did I need to know.

As I got into the book, I had one of those funny/weird Astrological moments. There I was bashing at the keyboard, having promised myself to get to a certain word-count that week and my brother-in-law (who is a Scorpio) phoned up to speak to my husband about my lovely mother-in-law who had recently died. He'd been sleepless that night wondering what to do about clearing their mother's house and when to 'sort-out' her ashes and he rang to say he'd decided what to do and when...so I looked at my Ephemeris and the days they'd decided to meet were when the Sun, the Moon, Mercury AND Venus were all going to be in the sign of Scorpio.

I had a little chuckle to myself.

I must point out my brother-in-law does not follow Astrology at all.

Then I thought: 'I wonder what the rising sign was when he called?', so I rang 1471 (which gives you a recorded message of when the call was made) and the rising sign or Ascendant was

Scorpio…and the Sun had just gone into Scorpio (about 35 mins not even a degree).

Brother-in-law doesn't usually ring in the morning, but this was an important phone call, for him, as it was about death (ashes), and as he has Moon in Capricorn practical things (the clearing of the house).

So what were the chances of a Scorpio ringing our house (I picked up the call) just when the Sun had reached Scorpio and the Ascendant was Scorpio and wanting to arrange something to do with death when the Sun, Moon, Mercury AND Venus were going to be in his sign?

I Love Astrology!

The title of this book was suggested to me by a lovely Pisces when I was grappling with the wording and she suggested How to *Win* the Trust of a Scorpio, when the original working title was *How to Trust a Scorpio*, which sort of implied that Scorpios aren't to be trusted…which is so far from the truth it's almost laughable.

Trust me, you can trust a Scorpio.

Bath, November 2011

Chapter One

The Sign

I like having a sense of what's going on in a room of people — sort of tapping into it, laying low, and feeling it all...In other words: Seeing without being seen; sensing without being sensed.
Female Scorpio

Scorpio is the 8th sign of the Zodiac and one that carries a lot of mystery and mis-understanding.

I went to school with a young lady to whom this book is dedicated and later on when she went into her career she told me she never mentioned what star sign she was at work, because she thought she'd get a negative response.

This can be rather true when you tell people you're a Scorpio. There is this sort of 'knowing' look you get and people take a few steps further away from you.

Here's a young lady called Tamsin talking about her sign:

It's the sense of identity that being a Scorpio gives you. We definitely stand for 'something' although that 'something' varies from very positive to completely negative... When you say you're a Scorpio, there's usually a physical reaction from the person you're saying it to — either they step back slightly or they move closer, curious to know more about this mysterious Scorpio in front of them. We're not a 'wishy-washy' sign! I don't mind the negative reactions, finding them amusing rather than anything else. Scorpios see things in black and white in any case.

Why is this?

It's amazing how telling people that you are a certain star sign (or more correctly astrological sign) can have this affect.

Most articles in books or especially on the Internet will make out Scorpio as being evil-planning, self-destructive, all-encompassing beings who are happy to ruin your life and steal your children away at the dead of night.

This simply isn't true.

So let's look at Scorpio in a different light and learn about their plus points before we discuss where-it-all-goes-wrong.

As I mentioned before, I'm an Astrologer that works 'on the front line' seeing people whose lives have imploded, who are: sad/stressed/unhappy/curious/worried, you name it, whatever emotion you can think of, I've probably seen a client suffering from it. And to further clarify; I will also have, in my own life, experienced something similar (as my first book *How to Survive a Pisces* reveals), as I'm a floppy Pisces.

Clients do not come and see me that have:

a) won the lottery
b) just got married
c) just been promoted

They tend to want to see me when their boyfriend/husband/wife/partner has left them, they've lost their job/health/house. When 'things' go wrong, they'll make an appointment.

I then have to act as counsellor, healer, wizard, friend, confidante, witness and we work together to find solutions that are do-able.

The clients that I see will complain about Scorpios (every sign complains about signs they've fallen foul to) in various different ways *depending on what sign **they** are*.

So let's find out a little about Scorpio, and how to make the best of the ones you know...and the ones you have yet to meet.

5

A Brief History of Astrology

Christopher McIntosh, a historian, tells us in his *The Astrologers and Their Creed* that Astrology was discovered in what is now called the Middle East — Iraq:

It was the priests of the kingdom of Babylonia who made the discovery, which set the pattern for the development of astronomy and of the zodiacal system of astrology that we know today. For many generations they had been meticulously observing and recording the movements of the heavenly bodies. Finally they had, by careful calculation, discovered that there were besides the Sun and the Moon, five other visible planets which moved in established courses through the sky. These were the planets that we now call Mercury, Venus, Mars, Jupiter and Saturn.

The discovery which these priest-astronomers made was a remarkable one, considering how crude were the instruments with which they worked. They had no telescopes, nor any of the complicated apparatus, which astronomers use today. But they did have one, big advantage. The area, next to the Persian Gulf, on which their kingdom lay, was blessed with extremely clear skies. In order to make full use of this advantage they built towers on flat areas of country and from these were able to scan the entire horizon.

These priests lived highly secluded lives in monasteries usually adjacent to the towers. Every day they observed the movements of the heavenly spheres and noted down any corresponding earthly phenomena from floods to rebellions. Very early on they had come to the conclusion that the laws which governed the movements of the stars and planets also governed events on Earth. The seasons changed with the movements of the Sun, therefore, they argued, the other heavenly bodies must surely exercise a similar influence...

In the beginning the stars and planets were regarded as

being actual gods. Later, as religion became more sophisticated, the two ideas were separated and the belief developed that the god 'ruled' the corresponding planet.

Gradually, a highly complex system was built up in which each planet had a particular set of properties ascribed to it. This system was developed partly through the reports of the priests and partly though the natural characteristics of the planets. Mars was seen to be red in colour and was therefore identified with the god Nergal, the fiery god of war and destruction.

Venus, identified by the Sumerians as their goddess Inanna, was the most prominent in the morning, giving birth as it were, to the day. She therefore became the planet associated with the female qualities of love, gentleness and reproduction.

The observation of the stars by the Sumerians was mostly a religious act. The planets were their gods and each visible object was associated with an invisible spiritual being that judged their actions, blessed them with good fortune or sent them tribulations. [1]

Astrology was therefore born out of careful observation and also a desire by the Sumerians to add meaning to their lives. As first, it was for a practical purpose, to help their crops, and then it developed into one that was spiritual and thousands of years later Astrology is still with us.

Definition of Astrology

Astrology is the study of the planets but not in the astronomical sense. Astrologers look at the planets and record where they are from the viewpoint of the Earth and divide the sky into 12 equal portions. Those portions start at the Spring Equinox of 0° Aries. We use astronomical information but the difference between astronomy and astrology is that astrologers use this astronomical information for a different purpose. Originally, astronomers and astrologers were the same species but as science progressed astronomers broke away and focused only on the planets themselves not on their meaning. Astrologers believe that we are all connected.

'As above, so below'

Just as we are all connected as beings from the same human race, astrologers believe we are all connected in some way to everything around us.

Pluto

Each sign of the Zodiac has a planet that 'looks after it'. We call it their 'ruler'. The Sun looks after Leo and the Moon looks after Cancer. The ruling planet to Scorpio is called Pluto and he's got a bit of a chequered history.

The Pisces who searched for Pluto and the Aquarius who found it

Percival Lowell the astronomer who was a Pisces, (Aries Ascendant, Sun in the 11th, Moon in Capricorn and who had Pluto in the sign of Taurus in his first house!) searched for Pluto for most of his life and sadly died before it was discovered.

Clyde Tombaugh, Sun Aquarius, (Moon Gemini) was a 24 year old researcher at the lab that was named after Percival: the Lowell Observatory. He actually discovered Pluto by taking a series of electronic wide-view photographs using an astrograph *near* the place in the sky that Percival had spent his time searching.

The planet was named Pluto by 11 year old Venetia Burney, Sun Cancer, (Moon Leo) after her dad read aloud an article about its discovery from *The Times* newspaper. She was very interested in Greek and Roman myths and legends at the time and as she said in an interview with the BBC in 2006:

"...it is extremely lucky that the name was there. There were practically no names left from classical mythology. Whether I thought about the dark and gloomy Hades, I'm not sure." [2]

The discovery was made in 1930, and Astrologers had to rethink their rulership of the signs, as at that point, they were only using the known nine 'planets': Sun, Moon, Mercury, Venus, Mars, Jupiter, Saturn, Uranus and Neptune.

Just to be clear a planet is a 'heavenly body' that orbits around the Sun, so technically the Moon isn't a planet as it orbits the Earth and the Sun isn't a planet either, it's a star but in Astrology we use the term planet to mean the bits we use from Sun to Pluto.

The Astronomical View of Pluto

Pluto is 3.6 billion miles away from the Earth and is smaller than our Moon, being 2,400km in diameter compared to our Moon at 3,474 km. Its orbit is egg-shaped so it doesn't go round the Sun in the same way as we do, and varies how far away it is from us here on Earth. NASA reckons that the surface of Pluto is very cold, over 375 degrees below zero and it takes 248 years for Pluto to go around the Sun. 3

The Astrological View of Pluto

It took a few years for Astrologers to get the hang of this new planet.

Margaret E Hone wrote in her *The Modern Text Book of Astrology*:

"This planet, less understood than any other at the time of writing (1950), has been known to astrologers for only twenty years"

but even she pointed out that it might be connected with:

"the growth of psychology"'

and that:

"Pluto was the god of the underworld, so the connection with what is submerged is seen."

By the 1970's Pluto was a little more understood by Astrologers and in his *Astrology and the Modern Psyche* by Dane Rudyar in 1976, he talks about Pluto in more detail:

Plutonian dreams may be the reflection upon the waking consciousness of real steps taken in inner unfoldment and soul growth-or, negatively, they reveal the pain or despair of the soul who has (at least temporarily) failed, and perhaps they show the abyss ahead and the dark presences that fill those abysmal depths.

Stirring stuff! Sounds kind of scary though. Not too sure, I'd want to have dreams like that too frequently.

By the 1980's Pluto was now part of the Astrological community's psyche as it worked its way through the sign of Scorpio the sign it rules. We had embraced 'his' energies and were getting more 'in tune' with how to deal with his negative side.

Jeff Green wrote in 1985 in his *Pluto: The Evolutionary Journey of the Soul*:

From a purely psychological point of view, Pluto correlates to the deepest emotional security patterns in all of us... Our lessons, or evolutionary intent described by Pluto's polarity point, are not known. They are the unknown, the uncharted...and therefore challenges our security at the deepest possible level — the Soul, our core.

But solutions were offered and practical help suggested by Donna Cunningham who writes so eloquently in her *Healing Pluto Problems* in 1986:

Pluto has its positive side too, and you can uplevel the energy of this planet from destructive to constructive. Pluto rules psychology and self-analysis, so you can purge yourself of the past by looking deep within and confronting yourself honestly. Pluto is the planet of rebirth, of healing and transformation. You can claim a new life for yourself, a joyful freedom from guilt and resentment, if you direct attention to recognizing and changing these patterns.

By 1989, Astrologers had got well into the swing of Pluto and were writing about how to 'deal' with Pluto transits, as opposed to having Pluto in the birth chart.

In *The Gods of Change, Pain, Crisis and the Transits of Uranus, Neptune and Pluto* Howard Sasportas wrote:

People tend to be afraid of Pluto transits, and they have a right to be, for we are dealing here with the god of death, whose domain is the dark and shadowy underworld. Transiting Pluto often brings us painfully into contact with death. In some cases this can mean a literal death-our own or that of someone close to us-but more usually these transits correspond to psychological deaths or 'ego-deaths': the death of a part of us, the death of ourselves as we know ourselves.

Then humour started to appear in Astrology with Bil Tierney, who is a Scorpio himself, writing the wonderful *Alive and Well with Pluto, Transits of Power and Renewal* in 1999:

Some astrologers put a rosy spin on a word that gets casually tossed about — "transformation" — thinking of it mainly in terms of the inspiring caterpillar-to-butterfly motif, but never the frightening human-to-werewolf scenario. However, if the transformative process was all that simple and clear-cut, Pluto wouldn't really be Pluto.

For 76 years, Pluto was the ninth planet from the Sun, and then in August 2006 it was 'demoted' by the astronomical authorities to the new status of Dwarf Planet.

This however, didn't stop Astrologers from using the planet in their calculations. They'd spent more than 70 years using him in birth charts and calculations, and they weren't going to be stopped.

Here's Jenni Harte writing about the 'new definition' of Pluto in September 2006 in the Astrological Association of Great Britain's publication *Transit*:

> *Following the New Moon of 23 August 2006 at 0 Virgo 31, the International Astronomical Union (IAU) gave us something huge to chew on…and you all know by now…Pluto's been demoted! Talk about change, this completely redefines our solar system, a big deal even if you aren't an astrologer!* [4]

And ends with:

> *Will I stop using Pluto in my astrological musings, I will not!*

I'm in agreement with Jenni on this one. Pluto is too interesting to ignore and matches Scorpio-ness quite adequately thank you.

Life and Death

When someone who is a Scorpio is in what I call their 'power' they can achieve great things. I know a number of people that work in social services as social workers, care assistants, care home managers (I'd love to do some research to find out how many matrons and managers of nursing/care/elderly homes are Scorpios) and they're dealing everyday with 'life and death' issues. And it suits them because they're not afraid of death.

So, what qualities do Astrologers say that Scorpio's have?

The four I'm going to discuss now are: Deep, Loyal, Secretive and Controlling. We will come onto Trust in a later chapter.

Deep

all that no-one sees

you see

what's inside of me

every nerve that hurts you heal

deep inside of me

you don't have to speak — I feel

Bjork 5.

What do we as humans mean when we say someone is 'deep'? My handy dictionary defines deep as: 'extending far down on or in from top or surface or edge'...and deep feelings as: 'fully absorbed or overwhelmed'.

If we were to play opposites here, we could say that Scorpio energy is not fluffy, superficial or light-hearted. I'd be more likely to say those were Gemini qualities.

Here is a young lady describing what being a Scorpio means for her:

I like having a sense of what's going on in a room of people — sort of tapping into it, laying low, and feeling it all. Although there have been times in my life when this feeling has been too strong (as a teen mostly), paralyzing me while I'm feeling too much! In other words: Seeing without being seen; sensing without being sensed.

She clearly describes how during her teens these feelings had paralysed her.

Let's go back to the dictionary definition above: fully absorbed or overwhelmed.

Now you're not going to feel 'fully absorbed or overwhelmed' if you're skimming the surface of something. You have to go deep.

So what do we actually mean when we say a Scorpio is deep?

We mean that they will focus on, and become 'as one with' whatever they are doing. They don't skim over the surface or flit around; they will go further and take themselves with what they do.

I'll give you an example.

I've had to deal a lot with social services over the last few years as my mother became too old to look after my youngest sister who has Down's Syndrome (I mentioned her in my book *How to Cheer up a Capricorn* as she is that sign).

I then started to come across a lot of Scorpios. They like working with people on the fringes of society. They like being motivated with a sense of purpose in the work they do and they also can work for long periods without supervision and are capable of dealing with sad/upsetting/tense situations that would put the fear of God into more fluffy signs. A number of social workers I came across were Scorpio. The manager of unit in the nursing home where my sister went is a Scorpio and I knew she was in safe hands when I found out his sign. They also have jobs in funeral parlours, or with the bereaved. They can work in incredibly intensely emotional places and are calm and collected in that work.

To me, that's deep. That takes a deep personality to want to work with people that are disadvantaged in some way, that are 'at the mercy' of life.

A lady came to my house one day who was training to be a social worker at our local University and she came to do what's called a care assessment. She asked all the right questions, was polite and gentle, kept on-track and didn't deviate from her task, which was to fill out her forms and get a 'feel' of how things were...and as she was leaving I asked her what sign she was.

"Scorpio," she said "Why?'... "Just curious," I said. She didn't ask any more questions, and off she went.

That's a Scorpio.

Accepting of how things are. She didn't, as some other signs might do, jump back at me with millions of questions. She just answered my question and left it at that.

Super!

The point I am making is a Scorpio will always focus on the task in hand. They won't multi-task. They will do one thing at a time. Do it well or not at all. Put all their life and soul into that task and will do it deeply.

Michel Gauquelin a French scientist spent 14 years proving an aspect of Astrology that he called The Mars Effect. He took the known birth data of 1553 French sports champions and found that Mars was significant in their birth charts. Mars is associated in Astrology with action, aggression and energy. He said,

"I have evidence, for instance, that Mars is prominent for military leaders and sports champions, more than just by pure chance. It's not Venus or some other planet, but Mars."

When interviewed by Michael Erlewine from The Matrix Astrology Software in January 1989 he said,

"Without the real hope, or the deep feeling that some theory would be found positively, I would probably never have continued." [6]

What drove him on to be ridiculed and mercilessly questioned by his scientific contemporaries? What made him continue to research and publish his results? What also resulted in him taking his own life?

Intensity and depth.

I expect, what also kept him going was his Leo Ascendant (look at me!) and Moon in Sagittarius (believe me!), but we'll come on to those other parts of a chart later.

Whatever job a Scorpio decides to do or have, they will put their whole self into it, and 'become' that occupation.

I also know a few white witches and women who work with

the Earth that are Scorpio. I won't name them as I haven't asked their permission to be included in this book but the two that come to mind have spent their whole lives doing what they do. They know their subject really well. Live it and breathe it. Their whole lives revolve around the world they've created. They're not pretending to do what they do. They are their work, and their work is their life. The two things can't be separated.

Once a Scorpio has made up their mind to do something, that's what they'll do. It would have to take some terrible circumstances for them to want to change their Life Path as they're what we call a Fixed Sign. These are the signs that don't like change:

Taurus, Leo and Scorpio are Fixed and they will only make changes after volcanic-like eruptions.

Think of the actress Jodie Foster and her performance in *The Silence of the Lambs* you can't get more 'deep' than she does in that film.

Loyal

Bless us, if it may be, in all our innocent endeavours.
If it may not, give us the strength to encounters that which is to come,
that we be brave in peril, constant in tribulation, temperate in wrath,
and in all changes of fortune, and, down to the gates of death,
loyal and loving one to another.
From Prayers Written at Vailima
Robert Louis Stevenson

My dictionary defines Loyal as: faithful, steadfast in allegiance...and I think describes Scorpio very well.

What makes a Scorpio more likely to remain faithful is their Fixed-Sign tendency. If you're someone who is focused, intense and deep, you will be more able to stick with something or someone than a person who is fickle and changeable.

Billie Jean King (Capricorn Asc Moon in Libra) the US tennis star wrote in 2010 after 49 years of coming to Wimbledon:

Today I was honored to meet Queen Elizabeth II. The Queen thanked me for being loyal to Wimbledon and we talked briefly about the role tennis plays in so many lives, including how it is a life sport for people of all ages and abilities.

She made her first appearance in 1961 age 17 and was still competing in 1983. That's over 22 years of professional work, which was then followed by being employed as a sports commentator. She stuck not only with the same field of work, but the same competition ground!

Margaret Atwood is a Canadian author, novelist and poet (Gemini Asc, Moon in Aquarius) and when asked about her creative self and her political self she replied,

"As an artist your first loyalty is to your art. Unless this is the case, you're going to be a second-rate artist."

And her writing is impressive. She's authored over 13 novels, 21 poetry books, 10 non-fiction titles and numerous children's books and short fiction. I've only written four books (this is my fifth) and already it feels an enormous task. I can't imagine writing as much as she has. It boggles the mind. And it takes a loyalty to an idea to be able to follow-through, which clearly Margaret has.

Joni Mitchell the superb singer/songwriter wrote in her song 'Stay in Touch' :

This is really something
People will be envious...
...Stay in touch.
In touch
Part of this is permanent
Part of this is passing
So we must be loyal and wary
Not to give away too much

This describes the Scorpio dilemma. Thinking people will be envious and that *because* things are both permanent and passing, she must stay loyal and wary. Loyal to her feelings? Loyal to the love? This isn't blind loyalty like being a member of a political party or a club, but loyal as in true to the 'self' and that part of the Scorpio that wants things unchanging and everlasting.

All three of these examples are to illustrate that Scorpio will be loyal to, those things that they have given themselves to and have devoted themselves to and that are *part* of themselves.

Secretive

There is something infinitely appealing about secrets. Some are easy to keep, some can never be revealed but it's one of those words that everyone responds to including our friend Scorpio.

Just the word 'secret' conjures up good and bad ideas. On Amazon if you do a title search for just the word secret, over 126,000 books turn up with the word 'secret' in the title.

That's a lot of books.

What is it about Scorpio that makes the word secret so compelling?

Here's a young Scorpio lady talking about this very subject:

...'Secrecy' and 'Mystery'... All Scorpios I've ever met are absolutely fascinated by these. And I've noticed that we always gravitate towards each other — for me, it has become almost a magnetic, unsaid attraction (I don't mean physical attraction — it's very intangible). A majority of my close friends are fellow Scorpios and I've always said it's because a) only a Scorpio understands another one and b) a lot of people are either scared of us or put off by our intensity.

There is another young lady who, as far as I know, isn't into Astrology. In fact, she's a research scientist and her name is Dr Brooke Magnanti. Her specialist areas are developmental neurotoxicology and cancer epidemiology. She has a PhD in informatics, epidemiology and forensic science and works at the Bristol Initiative for Research of Child Health at Bristol University. She is part of a research team investigating the 'mechanisms of placental transfer and toxicity of chemicals to which the mother may be exposed during pregnancy'. [7]

While studying for her PhD at Sheffield University she moved to London and from 2003 to late 2004 worked as a prostitute via a London escort agency.

She said she got to the point where she *"didn't have quite enough money"* for the rent and because of a relative who had a drug habit and became a streetwalker, she knew she'd be able to earn a living that didn't *"require a great deal of training or investment to get started, that's cash in hand"* and would leave her spare time to work on her studies.

The difference between this particular young lady and others in her profession was that she also wrote about her experiences in an on-line blog *Belle de Jour, Diary of a London Call Girl* and kept her identity secret until she came clean in a interview with the *Sunday Times* in November 2009.[8]

She is now married and living in Fort William in Scotland.

The point I am making here is that this young lady made a living out of being secretive, not so much out of her occupation. The suspense of 'who she was' kept the press amused for quite a while.

That is a truly Scorpio experience. Sex, secrets and being in control.

Controlling

What do we mean when we say a Scorpio is controlling? What is control? Back to my faithful dictionary.

Control: power of directing or restraining. So a Scorpio will want to direct, or restrain 'things' or 'people'.

Barbara is a Scorpio with Moon in Leo and is in her late

twenties and works as a waitress in a ski resort in Switzerland. She contacted me because of my Indigo Birth Chart research and told me a little about herself. I asked her what her views are on control and this is her reply:

I feel I try to control things on a subconscious level, like peoples inclinations. I do it "with my mind" or through intention. I have had to learn not to get hurt or cranky when people don't do what I expect. Learning to "relax and allow" has been an important lesson for me to learn. Sometimes this control is very good — the ability to focus so clearly on making something specific happen. Sometimes it undermines me because I am so focused on something that isn't meant to be, like a relationship or having dinner before 6 or whatever. Allowing the flow of the universe to guide me is a major blessing.

She's aware that her ability to 'control' depends on whether or not what she wants is for the better good and it's a good example of how a Scorpio wants to work on a deeper level than just verbal or physical.

She continues:

Of course there are also opposite times where I totally let go of control and fall into a kind of waiting, which sometimes feels like stagnation but probably isn't. Makes me think of the scorpion sitting for hours in one position waiting to strike.

Yes! The Scorpion can wait for hours before it strikes...and motionless it is too!

Chapter Two

How to Make a Chart

Using Astrology is like building-up a painting. You start with the outline (the chart) and add some buildings or people (the planets) with a smattering of landscape (the houses) some perspective and then colour.

Only when you see all of it together can you make a judgement. And what seems nice to one person will be horrible to someone else. It is the same with Astrologers.

Some (like me) like the Equal House system, because all the houses are the same size and uniform. Others prefer the Placidus system because they like the fact that the Midheaven is at the 12 o'clock position and makes more 'sense'. I don't do sense that often, I'm a Pisces don't forget! But basically, the planets and their position in the sky at the moment of your birth are translated into a circle with 12 segments.

Each one of the segments represents a different area of life and each planet can be in any one of the 12 signs from Aries to Pisces.

Before you start, you will need three pieces of information.

The date your Scorpio was born, the place they were born and most importantly, the time.

The general dates for a Scorpio Sun sign are the 24th October to the 22nd November. I say general because every year those dates change a teeny bit. For instance, in 2012 the Sun leaves Scorpio on the 21st November because the orbit of the Sun doesn't match exactly the days in a month, as some months have more days.

It also depends where in the world you were born, as someone born in Australia will have a different chart to someone born in Glasgow, so don't rely only on the dates above. Check and re-check before you decide the person in your life is actually a Scorpio.

I have a lovely story to tell you about real person in my life. I can't give you too much info, but take this as true.

She originally gave me her date and time of birth as being in 23rd October and born at 1am in the morning. This made her a Libra, with Leo Ascendant and Moon in Libra. Years passed, and then one day when I was reading her birth data out to her, she said, "No, I was born in the afternoon". So I asked her to check with her parents again and she came back with her time as being 1pm in the afternoon.

No!

All these years I'd been reading her chart as a double Libra, when in fact she was a Scorpio, and not only a Scorpio but a double-Scorpio with Sun and Moon in Scorpio and now a Sagittarius Ascendant.

DOH!

She also was very concerned when she read anything about Scorpios as she didn't see herself as secretive or nasty and jealous, which she isn't, so this book has been written to help her and others like her, who really, truly don't see themselves in such a negative light.

Making an Equal House Chart

To make your Scorpio's chart, go to http://www.astro.com and make an account then go to the Free Horoscopes section and scroll down and use the special part of their site, called the 'Extended Chart Selection'.

You've already inputted all your data, which will be shown in the box at the top where your name is.

Scroll down the page again and under the section marked 'Options' you'll see a box that says 'House System' and in the box it will say 'default'.

Now make sure you *change the box to say* 'equal'. The default system is called Placidus and all the houses will be different sizes and for a beginner that's just too confusing.

We're going to make the chart of Cheiro, a famous Victorian Palmist. He was born on 1st November 1886 in Dublin, Ireland at 10.53am in the morning.

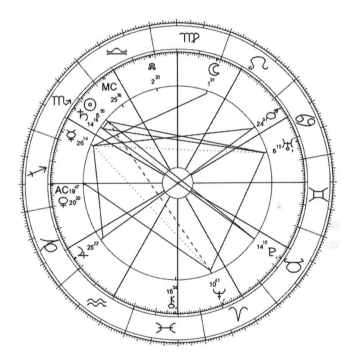

This is Cheiro's chart. The lines in the centre of the chart are either easy or challenging mathematical associations between each planet in the chart, but for our purposes, ignore them.

The houses are numbered 1-12 in an anti-clockwise order. We will be learning about them in Chapter Five.

We only want three pieces of information:

The sign of the Ascendant, the sign the Moon is in and the house number that the Sun is in.

This is the abbreviation for the Ascendant: AC, which we will learn about that in Chapter Three.

This is the symbol for the Sun: ☉

This is the symbol for the Moon: ☽ we will learn about that in Chapter Four.

These are the shapes representing the signs. They are called glyphs. The glyph for Scorpio looks like the letter M with an arrow at the bottom.

Aries ♈
Taurus ♉
Gemini ♊
Cancer ♋
Leo ♌
Virgo ♍
Libra ♎
Scorpio ♏
Sagittarius ♐
Capricorn ♑
Aquarius ♒
Pisces ♓

The Elements

To understand your Scorpio fully, you must take into account which Element their Ascendant and Moon are in.

Each sign of the Zodiac has been given an element that it operates under: Earth, Air, Fire and Water. I like to think of them as operating at different 'speeds'.

The **Earth** signs are **Taurus**, **Virgo** and **Capricorn**. The Earth Element is stable, grounded and concerned with practical matters. A Scorpio with a lot of Earth in their chart works best at a very slow, steady speed (I refer to these in the text as 'Earthy').

The **Air** signs are **Gemini, Libra** and **Aquarius** (who is the 'Water-carrier' *not* a water sign). The Air element enjoys ideas, concepts and thoughts. It operates at a faster speed than Earth, not as fast as Fire but faster than Water and Earth. Imagine them as being medium speed.

The **Fire** signs are **Aries, Leo** and **Sagittarius**. The Fire element likes action, excitement and can be very impatient. Their speed is *very* fast (I refer to these as Firey i.e. Fire-Sign).

The **Water** signs are **Cancer, Scorpio** and **Pisces**. The Water element involves feelings, impressions, hunches and intuition. They operate faster than Earth but not as fast as Air. A sort of slow–medium speed.

Chapter Three

The Ascendant

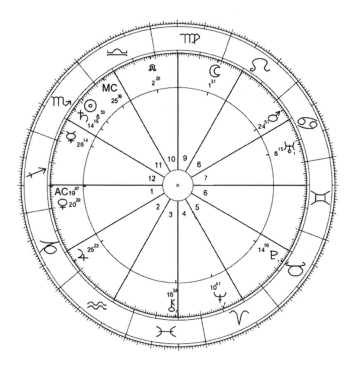

Name: ♂ Cheiro
born on Th., 1 November 1866
in Dublin, IRE
6w15, 53n20

Time: 10:53 a.m.
Univ.Time: 11:18
Sid. Time: 13:35:04

This is the birth chart of Count Louis Hamon better known under his pseudonym of 'Cheiro'. He was born in Ireland and christened William John Warner but changed his name when he set up in practice in the UK. He was a famous Victorian Palmist who wrote a number of books on Palmistry, Numerology and Astrology. He eventually moved to Hollywood and died there in 1936. In his day, he read for people like Mata Hari the exotic dancer who was executed as a spy, Oscar Wilde and his claim to fame King of England, Edward VII who incidentally had almost the same chart as him. Both of them had Sag Asc and both had Moon in Virgo. I mentioned how I learned to read palms from his books in my first book *How to Survive a Pisces*.

If you look closely at the above image you will see the letters AC19 on the left hand side of the circle just over half-way through the sign of Sagittarius, which has a glyph that looks like an arrow. That's the astrological shorthand for the sign of Sagittarius. This means that Cheiro had a Sagittarius Ascendant.

That's all you need to know for the moment. The sign the Ascendant is in.

As it's determined by the exact time of birth, as opposed to the date of birth, which gives us the Sun sign, it's a very important part of the birth chart. The moment you became 'alive' to your surroundings.

So, what's an Ascendant?

Astronomically it the sign that was 'rising' on the eastern horizon at the exact time of birth. How you 'come into' the world.

We look at it as the way we view the world, the specs we wear, how we experience life, maybe even the coat we wear. It's not 'who' we are, that's the Sun sign, and it mostly is how other people see us too.

Someone with a Fire sign Ascendant will tackle life in a more speedy way than someone with an Earth sign Ascendant. It's a sort of vision filter.

So Cheiro, who we know as our friend the Scorpio, had Sagittarius Rising/Ascending and was therefore interested in all things 'foreign', other cultures, spirituality and philosophy: the meaning of life.

Your Ascendant can be any sign of the Zodiac. It all depends on your birth time so if you don't know the time, ignore this chapter as the Ascendant changes sign every two hours.

Here are the Ascendants through the signs for our friend the Scorpio with little examples and quotes from famous Scorpios whose chart we know are correct.

Aries Ascendant

My opportunities are still vast and fantastic.
Bo Derek

As the first sign of the zodiac, Aries is seen as the leader sign. It's assertive, brave and goes boldly where angels fear to tread. As a fire sign, it operates swiftly and confidently. It has oodles of self-belief and will just ignore you if you disagree with them.

Taurus Ascendant

I need something truly beautiful to look at in hotel rooms.
Vivien Leigh

Taurus is ruled by the loving planet Venus and enjoys all of life's romances and pleasures. It is sensual, earthy and grounded. The physical body is a major concern and there is a need to keep it satisfied with good food, good sex and maybe even the occasional chocolate treat.

Gemini Ascendant

Words are as strong and powerful as bombs, as napalm.
Dorothy Day

Airy, flighty, chatty Gemini as a rising sign for Scorpio makes for an interesting combination. It cleverly disguises that deep Scorpio energy by being interested in all forms of communication especially speech and the written word.

Cancer Ascendant

You could write a song about some kind of emotional problem you are having, but it would not be a good song, in my eyes, until it went through a period of sensitivity to a moment of clarity. Without that moment of clarity to contribute to the song, it's just complaining.
Joni Mitchell

As another water sign Cancer is sensitive to all emotions and feelings especially those that revolve around the family and children. Domestic concerns such as cooking and keeping house are enjoyed rather than rejected. For a Scorpio though it can double the tendency to moodiness.

Leo Ascendant

I just wanted to have a hit, I just wanted to be like those people on the radio.
Art Garfunkel

Sunny Leo likes to shine, to see and be seen. It is not a shy sign and loves adoration, red carpets and an appreciative audience. For a Scorpio this can cause inner confusion: on the one hand wanting recognition, and on the other secrecy and obscurity.

Virgo Ascendant

A man will give up almost anything except his suffering.
John Cleese

Of all the signs most likely to worry Virgo tops the list. Incessant, repetitive thoughts and a deep concern for health and healing can create angst. On the positive side, Virgo is about order and categorization and the ability to be specific and exact.

Libra Ascendant

Johnny and me. We were joined at the hip.
Cleo Laine

Libra is the other sign ruled by Venus and makes close personal relationships, an absolute necessity. I tend to 'prescribe' a partner for people with this ascendant as otherwise they feel lost and alone. There are also issues to do with fairness and balance as Libra is represented by the scales of justice.

Scorpio Ascendant

I believe in a zone of privacy.
Hillary Clinton

Don't come too close uninvited. Doubling up the Scorpio energies means this person will put up an impenetrable wall to unwanted intervention. Secretive, intense, maybe even jealous on a bad day but certainly focused, blindingly honest and truthful. And if they don't like you, you cease to exist. You are 'nothing'.

Sagittarius Ascendant

During my stay in India, I was permitted by some Brahmans...to examine and make extracts from an extraordinary book...which they regarded as almost sacred.
Cheiro

The expansive, outgoing and philosophical Sagittarius Ascendant will make a Scorpio more capable of making mistakes and shrugging them off. They want to reach as high and as far as possible with their arrows of perception. They will also tell you as it is, no holds barred.

Capricorn Ascendant

Victory is fleeting. Losing is forever.
Billie Jean King

A more serious sign but one that is highly compatible with Scorpio energies Earthy Capricorn will see the world with reality specs firmly in place. The downside can be a tendency towards a bleaker viewpoint; however they are capable of accepting great responsibility.

Aquarius Ascendant

Is there no way out of the mind?
Sylvia Plath

Airy Aquarius needs to be mentally free, and will not enjoy limitation, rules or regulations. Inventive, cerebral and certainly a cooler sign for a Scorpio to absorb it can create some discord and mental struggles. On the plus side, there is plenty of discussion, thought and musing.

Pisces Ascendant

A sanctuary becomes a hiding place, and that's not a benefit to anybody.
Demi Moore

Another Water sign, Pisces increases the emotional sensitivity for Scorpio. As the last sign of the Zodiac and one more prone to absorb other people's troubles this Asc can become the emotional sponge. Daily meditation practice helps, as does the concept that not every wrong can be healed every time, all the time.

Chapter Four

The Moon

If the Sun in Astrology represents our 'ego', who we are, then the Moon, as in real life reflects back the energy of the Sun and becomes in Astrology our subconscious, or our emotional self. When the Sun and Moon are at odds with each other, it can result in saying one thing...and doing another, so getting an understanding of your Scorpio's Moon sign is a great help.

The symbol for the Moon is the half-crescent so look for it in your chart you have made.

Remember the Elements too, as the Scorpio Sun is a Water sign and if their Moon is in a Fire sign say of Aries, Leo or Sagittarius, they will go into 'action mode' every now and then and you'll be standing there wondering a) where all that energy came from and b) what happened to that emotional, deep person you were talking to yesterday.

As the Moon represents our emotions, getting an understanding of them makes things a lot easier, especially if life is getting heated or out-of-hand.

I sometimes think life would be a whole lot easier if we didn't have emotions, then I think how dull life would be and also how unimaginative. But, like with everything, getting a balance is the best way to go.

Too much emotion and we're trapped in our feelings, worn out by grief, worry and despair. Not enough emotion and we miss feeling happy, elated or joyous. Getting the balance right means we can feel at peace, which is a jolly nice feeling.

In our example, Cheiro had his Moon in the sign of Virgo, so he was very good at categorising and recalling information. He read hands for a living for over 40 years and by the time he died, he'd amassed a collection of thousands of prints.

The Dr Bach Flower Essences

In 1933, Dr Edward Bach a medical doctor and homeopath published a little booklet called *The Twelve Healers and Other Remedies*. His theory was that if the emotional component a person was suffering from was removed, their 'illness' would also disappear. I tend to agree with this kind of thinking as most illnesses (except being hit by a bus) are preceded by an unhappy event or an emotional disruption that then sets into place the body getting out of sync. Removing the emotional issue and bringing a bit of stability into someone's life, when they are having a hard time, can improve their overall health so much that wellness resumes.

Knowing which Bach Flower Essence can help certain worries and upsetments gives you and your Scorpio more control over your lives. I recommend the essences a lot in my practice if I feel a certain part of a person's chart is under stress...and usually it's the Moon that needs help. The essences describe the negative aspects of the character, which are focused on during treatment. This awareness helps reverse those trends, so when our emotional selves are nice and comfortable, we can then face each day with more strength.

I've quoted Dr Bach's actual words for each sign.

To use the Essences take 2 drops from the stock bottle and put it into a glass of water and sip. I tend to recommend putting them into a small water bottle, and sipping them through-out the day, at least 4 times. For young children, do the same.

Remember to seek medical attention if symptoms don't get better and/or seek professional counselling.

Aries Moon

I don't think we realize just how fast we go until you stop for a minute and realize just how loud and how hectic your life is, and how easily distracted you can get.
Meg Ryan

As a Fire sign, and first sign of the Zodiac, Aries is all about 'me'. They will need to feel that the world revolves around their feelings, so not so good at sharing or compromise. It has the added benefit though of being completely truthful, so if you ask an Aries Moon how they are feeling and they tell you, they're being totally honest.

Bach Flower Essence Impatiens:

> *"Those who are quick in thought and action and who wish all things to be done without hesitation or delay."*

Taurus Moon

Taurus depends on its feelings and instincts to better understand the nature of physical reality.
Bil Tierney

Grounded in the reality of the Earth and all its pleasures, Taurus Moon will want nice tasty food, stable finances, and raunchy sex. Taste is important, as are the kinaesthetic senses of touch, so soft fluffy clothing, velvet/silk/satin and things that feel pleasant are incredibly important. They won't say No to good wine and chocolate either and as a slower sign will develop gradually. Don't rush them!

Bach Flower Essence Gentian:

> *"Those who are easily discouraged. They may be progressing well in the affairs of their daily life, but any small delay or hindrance to progress causes doubt and soon disheartens them."*

Gemini Moon

So curiosity, I think, is a really important aspect of staying young or youthful.
Goldie Hawn

Oh, the eternal child! Gemini never wants to grow old! This is the Moon sign of two options and opinions as they are astrological twins. They like discussion, argument, conversation and for things to be (as this is an Air sign) cerebral and swift. Short journeys are loved too.

Bach Flower Essence Cerato:

> *"Those who have not sufficient confidence in themselves to make their own decisions."*

Cancer Moon

Everyone discusses my art and pretends to understand, as if it were necessary to understand, when it is simply necessary to love.
Claude Monet

The Cancer Moon is happiest when they can feel their emotions, feel safe, nurtured, cuddled and snuggled. As Cancer is 'ruled' by the Moon, it's in its home sign. They can be cranky and moody but equally they will love deeply. They will also love mum/mom, the home and home delights and all things aged and traditional.

Bach Flower Essence Clematis:

> *"Living in the hopes of happier times, when their ideals may come true."'*

Leo Moon

It's funny when people say, 'I don't think Julia likes me.' Honey, if I don't like you, you're going to know about it.
Julia Roberts

When the Moon goes into Leo, things hot up. It's a cheery, optimistic Moon but ignore it at your peril! They love to bask in the glow of the love from their entourage, enjoy the red-carpet treatment, wince if you forget their name and love you if you thank them profusely for their kindness, which will be great.

Bach Flower Essence Vervain:

> *"Those with fixed principles and ideas, which they are confident are right."*

Virgo Moon

It's okay to be crazy, but don't be insane.
Puff Daddy

Here we have the sign that could get a degree in worrying. They worry about this, they worry about that, they then worry about worrying and so it goes on. On a good day, their powers of analysis and classification are a joy and they have an enormous memory for irrelevant information. They will happily dot every 'i' and cross every 't' and remind you that you said this and that on certain dates. Encyclopaedias and libraries are well starred too.

Bach Flower Essence Centuary:

> *"Their good nature leads them to do more than their own share of work and they may neglect their own mission in life."*

Libra Moon

I was a queen, and you took away my crown; a wife, and you killed my husband; a mother, and you deprived me of my children. My blood alone remains: take it, but do not make me suffer long.
Queen Marie Antoinette

This is the classic sign of indecision represented by the scales that form the sign of Libra. Should I do this? Or that? Their concerns will centre around close personal relationships and they are at their happiest with a ring on their finger and someone to love. Fairness and balance are also important.

Bach Flower Essence Scleranthus:

> *"Those who suffer from being unable to decide between two things, first one seeming right then the other."*

Scorpio Moon

I knew from the start I wanted the album to be bloody, physical and urgent.
Bjork

If you think of the colour deep, deep red, you'll get an idea of what it's like to have a Scorpio Moon. Deep feelings, deep thoughts and even deep resentments if they're frustrated in their desires. There are no half-measures. All or nothing. They will stick through thick and thin if they're on your side. They will stop at nothing if you're not. Not a combination to trifle with.

Bach Flower Essence Chicory:

> "They are continually correcting what they consider wrong and enjoy doing so."

Sagittarius Moon

If you are really sure that you are right, you have no fear from any kind of criticism. So, it's probably the only philosophy I got from my experiences.
Michel Gauquelin

As a Fire sign and one of the more swift-speed Moons, Sagittarius Moon wants to answer all of life's questions, or at least ask them and investigate them. Any sort of learning or teaching will keep them amused as will contact with foreign countries and other civilisations. On the downside, they love to 'be right' so be careful not challenge their beliefs too much.

This Essence comes under the heading 'Over-Sensitive to Influences and Ideas'.

Bach Flower Essence Agrimony:

> "They hide their cares behind their humor and jesting and try to bear their trials with cheerfulness."

Capricorn Moon

I grew up always treated like I was a foreigner, and had a non-Anglo name. But for me, those were the obstacles that made me stronger.
Ming-Na

Capricorn is ruled by strict Saturn, the planet of 'hard-knocks'. They will learn at an early age that life isn't always fluffy and fun. They will prefer serious subjects, sensible ideas and life built on firm foundations. They will also put up with more than any other sign and be stoic in how they tackle life's challenges.

Bach Flower Essence Mimulus:

> *"Fear of wordly things, illness, pain, accident, poverty, of dark, of being alone, of misfortune. They secretly bear their dread and do not speak freely of it to others."*

Aquarius Moon

> *I die adoring God, loving my friends, not hating my enemies, and detesting superstition.*
> Voltaire

Friendship with a capital 'F' rules Aquarius. For a Scorpio it reduces slightly their emotional deepness and allows weird and wonderful ideas and friendships to be born. Full of ideas and crazy thoughts they will draw you into their world-view, which is inclusive and utopian. Whether or not they are happy as a human is debateable. Spock from Star Trek comes to mind, but fun they certainly can be.

Bach Flower Essence Water Violet:

> *"For those who like to be alone, very independent, capable and self-reliant. They are aloof and go their own way."*

Pisces Moon

I do know that some Buddhists are able to attain peace of mind.
Martin Scorsese

As the last sign of the Zodiac and one that is supremely sensitive to fairies, angels, and all things spiritual and otherworldly, a Scorpio with Moon in Pisces will have a slightly longer road to travel to get to contentment. As the sign of the martyr, they can, on a bad day, imagine all the suffering in the world, which will make them feel weak and low. On a good day they will sense you are trying to reach them, imagine (correctly) how you are feeling and will 'be there' for you in this life and the next. Just make sure you guide them back to earth occasionally...

Bach Flower Essence Rock Rose:

"For cases where there even appears no hope or when the person is very frightened or terrified."

Chapter Five

The Houses

One of the most difficult things to explain to a newbie astrologer is what a 'house' is. I'll do my best to make some sense here, but please excuse me if I don't manage it.

A house is an astrological term for the division of the map of the heavens that we call a Birth chart or Horoscope.

Astrologers weren't content to just plot the paths of the planets, they also wanted to do more maths and divide things up. So they divided the circle of the chart into 12 equal portions.

I use a house system called Equal House but there are plenty of other ways of dividing a circle, as any cake cutter will tell you. The default system that most computer programmes and websites use is called Placidus but to me that looks a little strange as each house is a different size...and I like some order in my life and prefer things to be equal.

When they'd divided the circle up, they wanted those divisions to mean something and it's that meaning that I will be explaining.

The chart has to have a starting point, that's the Ascendant, which we talked about earlier...and the divisions are the houses, which represent different areas of life. And if a planet is in a certain house, it 'means' something else.

So having the Sun in the first house, which we will cover in a minute, means you'll be more assertive, more forceful maybe a bit more 'in your face' than someone with their Sun in the 12th house, who will be more likely to hide away from discovery.

The Ascendant and first house represents how we tackle life, the second house our finances and attitude to life and how we 'value' ourselves and so on round the circle anti-clockwise, or as they say in the US counter clockwise. I've only included what it means if the Scorpio Sun is in each house. There are nine other 'planets' we use in a chart and this book is too small to include all the different possibilities but knowing just the sign of the Ascendant, the sign of the Moon and where the Sun is located around the circle is a great starting point. In our example chart of Cheiro, his Sun is in the 11th house

This is where your average scientist switches off. How can something on a piece of paper or a map relate to anything personal in a human being?

Well, one way of looking at it is to think about how we are all part of the same cosmos. We all exist in the same Universe and as much as we think we don't influence each other, we do. When you're having a bad day because your car won't start, you'll be cross and grumpy and your partner will feel equally cross and grumpy, because you're moaning…and so on.

In Astrology we use the term 'as above, so below' in that what happens here on Earth is reflective of what happens in the heavens. It's not the same, it's similar.

Ancient Astrologers divided the map into a square, so it hasn't always been a circle. But the circle sort of stuck and that's where we are today. Twelve 'houses' each one representing an aspect of our lives from our 'self' to our friends and family, to our partner, our birth and death, our career, our work…all the way round to our spiritual self.

Interestingly enough, the 8th house, which represents death and birth is similar, but not the same as the energies of Scorpio, which is the 8th sign of the Zodiac.

Neat.

The First House, House of Personality

All action results from thought, so it is thoughts that matter.
Sai Baba

The first house is where we emerge into the world. Where things are immediate and active. Our birth. With the Sun here your Scorpio will be confident, able to tackle tasks quickly and decisively, confident and self-assured (depending on what sign the Moon is in). Less capable of sharing.

(Ascendant Scorpio or Libra)

The Second House, House of Money, Material Possessions and Self-Worth

If you knew how meat was made, you'd probably lose your lunch.
k. d. lang

The second house is all about our 'worth and value', so it can literally be money and possessions, as they have value or figuratively how much you are valued as a person. They will love food, massage, chocolate and good wine. Anything that can be physically enjoyed by the body. The Sun here makes your Scorpio more inclined to want to live in the physical real world and less likely to operate on abstract ideas.

(Ascendant Libra or Virgo)

The Third House, House of Communication & Short Journeys

He can who thinks he can, and he can't who thinks he can't. This is an inexorable, indisputable law.
Pablo Picasso

The third house represents our first words. If the first house is the baby, and the second the infant, the 3rd house is the toddler asking the eternal 'Why?' The Sun here makes the native enjoy chatting, writing, communicating and making short journeys. Siblings are also important and anything to do with making contact with others. So watch out for the phone-bill!

(Ascendant Virgo or Leo)

The Fourth House, House of Home, Family & Roots

I was determined to devote full time to my children. A child's need of his mother's love and care is as urgent and fundamental as that of a plant for sunshine and water.
Indira Ghandi

Sun in the 4th revolves around nurturing, the family and those things that make us feel homey and settled. It's also the house of our roots, so with the Sun here, there might be an interest in family history or distant relatives. The mothering instinct is well developed too.

(Ascendant Leo or Cancer)

The Fifth House, House of Creativity & Romance

For unflagging interest and enjoyment, a household of children, if things go reasonably well, certainly all other forms of success and achievement lose their importance by comparison.
Theodore Roosevelt

This is the house that is confident and likes to show-off. Creative? Yes. Dramatic? Also Yes. It is also equally about children and romance. Ignoring a 5th house Sun is not an option as they're likely to sulk. They will love attention, flattery and being noticed and will be warm and generous in return.

(Ascendant Cancer or Gemini)

The Sixth House, House of Work & Health

Go three days without water and you don't have any human rights. Why? Because you're dead. Physics and chemistry are things you just can't negotiate with. These are the laws of the physical world.
Margaret Atwood

As this is the house of health and healing and also strangely, work, a Scorpio Sun here will manifest as someone who likes to be busily sorting out their physical condition and getting stuck into the detail of life. Worry can also be a problem.

(Ascendant Gemini or Taurus)

The Seventh House, House of Relationships & Marriage

I believe wholeheartedly in marriage. I don't exclusively mean a marriage with a legal contract, but any relationship that constitutes a marriage because of the quality of their relationship.
Helen Reddy

The 7th house is all about marriage and close personal relationships. With the Sun here, being in a partnership will be top of the list. Being single weighs heavily, so dating will be uppermost. They will view their life through those relationships and will feel better when they have a ring on their finger or at the very least, someone special in their life.

(Ascendant Taurus or Aries)

The Eighth House, House of Life Force in Birth, Sex, Death & After-Life

Our love is so furious that we burn each other out.
Richard Burton

As this is the Scorpio Sun's 'natural' home as the 8th house is similar to the 8th sign: Scorpio, the Sun in this house will be 100 per cent Scorpio. Deep feelings, deep emotions, bottom-less and profound experiences. Life is lived with intensity with a capital 'I'. No half-measures here, everything moving at a fast furious pace.

(Ascendant Aries or Pisces)

The Ninth House, House of Philosophy & Long Distance Travel

Nothing is better for a young journalist than to go and write about something that other people don't know about. If you can afford to send yourself to some foreign part, I still think that's by far the best way to break in.
Tina Brown

When the Sun falls into the 9th house, there is the desire to travel as far as possible to exotic, foreign, different cultures. They're interested in and inspired by philosophy, religion, spirituality and any form of complex thinking. They want to know 'Why?' and love to question concepts.

(Ascendant Pisces or Aquarius)

The Tenth House, House of Social Identity & Career

My parents were extraordinary, as were their parents, so I come from a long line of family whose belief was. You can do it, but you have to work really hard—and you're not allowed to make excuses.
Condoleezza Rice

This is the house whereby 'others' will judge you, or you judge yourself by your ability to succeed. It is the worldly house and the Scorpio Sun here will want to rise above any humble begin-nings and 'better' themselves. Ambition will be paramount and

ruled by Saturn the hard-task-master, it might take some time to get there, but get there they must.
(Ascendant Aquarius or Capricorn)

The Eleventh House, House of Social Life & Friendships

I am one of those who think like Nobel, that humanity will draw more good than evil from new discoveries.
Marie Curie

Friendships are important in the 11th house as is altruistic purpose. They will enjoy working and being in groups more than being alone (depending on other chart factors) and can be a little distant in personal relationships because of this. Shared visions are appealing as is the desire to benefit humankind in some way.
(Ascendant Capricorn or Sagittarius)

The Twelfth House, House of Spirituality

I believe in a zone of privacy
Hillary Clinton

The Sun in the 12th house needs to have 'me' time away from others with space to just 'be'. Time spent alone, maybe in Nature, maybe locked in the bathroom/shower somewhere watery and where their emotions can be felt without interruption. If they were in a rock band, the 12th house Sun would be the bassist or rhythm guitarist, not the lead singer. They sense things more than they admit.
(Ascendant Sagittarius or Scorpio)

Chapter Six

The Difficulties

As I mentioned earlier, I work 'on the front line' with clients. They come to see me for a whole host of different reasons, unhappiness being the biggest. We can easily get to a state of unhappiness when our lives are full of tragedy, stress and unrealised expectations or ambition.

Scorpio clients only come and see me when those 'things' are really, *really* difficult. I'm very unlikely to see a Scorpio client who is still 'in control'. It's when that control has disappeared that they will make an appointment.

And they will very rarely tell me the true reason why they've come and I have to get deeply into their life situation and circumstances and they have to feel they can trust me, before they will ever tell me what's truly happening for them.

One thing you can't do when you're working with a Scorpio client, is give them a load of fluff and bluff. You have to be honest, maybe even painfully so, but it's this honesty that they will want to hear.

If they've got a Scorpio Ascendant too, I have to be *very* sure that they feel safe. I also make sure that they understand that what they tell me is confidential, that I won't be discussing what they've told me with anyone else, unless they are threatening to harm themselves or someone else. Then I might have to refer them on.

Now, if the client I am seeing is married/dating/related/friends with a Scorpio, things are a little different. Depending on what sign the friend or spouse or so forth may be, will determine how they're coping with what's happening. A Pisces is more likely to feel totally overwhelmed by events and want them to stop, while an Aries will be battling, fighting and generally giving as good as they've got, which won't work with a Scorpio...ever. Not even if they're a really polite one.

Here is Jacqueline, a double Aries with Sun and Moon in Aries (and Mars right on the Ascendant, but that's another story) talking about her ex husband's antics:

"At the beginning of our marriage, for example, a dry cleaner ruined an old jacket of his. He went on and on about this for hours, even talking about GASSING them!"

Not only did she stay with him after this, but she also had a baby with him.

It was interesting to hear her explanation of how and why she left:

"After 20 years of wondering why I called that experience into my life, here's what I finally decided: I needed to grow into the courage of Aries. And it wasn't until I no longer feared death that I found the courage to leave him. Sometimes I think it is a wonder I survived. One of his lawyers did not — he committed suicide."

No matter how you look at it, there has to be an awfully large amount of emotion going on, for situations like this to happen, and it's those emotions that need understanding and reining in, for both partners, before a solution can be found. So here are some everyday situations you might come across with your Scorpio and how to tackle them.

My Scorpio wants me to promise I'll do something.

If you want to be happy with the Scorpio in your life, don't agree to promise something you might change your mind about, or could easily not do.

Don't promise anything unless you are 100 per cent sure you

can deliver the results. And definitely don't promise undying love. Just state the facts.

Far too many relationships of all kinds have been destroyed by someone promising something to a Scorpio, then not being able to follow-through. It is one thing a Scorpio will rarely do themselves i.e. break a promise, so be careful you don't commit to a promise unless you can cross your heart that you will deliver the promised result. Might be better to agree to 'do your best' or 'make a start' or 'give it a go'. As always, it depends on what sign you are. If you're the chatty sort, be careful you don't say something you will later regret.

My Scorpio won't tell me everything/anything.

It's amazing how this upsets so many people. A Scorpio will only confide in/to you when they feel completely confident in not only your behaviour but your words and the feelings-in-between. No good putting them under the spotlight the minute they come home. Or asking what they did, or where they went.

That's their business.

They'll tell you when they're good and ready.

I had an Aquarius client with Moon in Scorpio who was married to a Scorpio with Moon in Aquarius. He'd barely put his foot through the door and she was onto him asking him where, when and why.

He just wanted to reconfigure, she wanted a complete breakdown of the day's events.

Now when the tables were turned and he asked her what she'd been up to, she went into meltdown and accused him of being suspicious and jealous. This went on for months and months.

Eventually, she let him get settled and rested and they talked later in the day when he'd had a chance to unwind.

When my client realised that by questioning her Scorpio she was assuming he couldn't be trusted (when he could) things settled down.

My Scorpio is so emotional I don't know how to cope with him/her.

This does cause a lot of angst to the Air signs. I saw a retired Gemini client in my practice who just couldn't get her newly retired Scorpio to see the world in the light and fluffy way that she so liked. She thought he was depressed.

She wanted to go out on little trips, visiting stately homes or concerts, he wanted to stay at home and do 'homey' things. This was causing her a great amount of worry. There she was being bright and breezy...there he was doing what he liked and not nibbling the bait. I suggested she just go and do all the things she loved to do and maybe, maybe her Scorpio man would accompany her sometimes. I did emphasise *sometimes*.

If your Scorpio gets emotional, just wait until the emotion passes. It will. Just like the thunderstorm that threatens to blow the roof off the house, eventually the wind dies down, the rain stops and things become quiet and settled. So it is with a Scorpio and their emotions. Don't try to stop them having emotions. They love the sense of excitement they bring them, the feeling of aliveness and being-ness. Of being in their bodies, of being a real, live human being. It can be quite a compelling, addictive trait, but it's one you will have to understand and respect in a Scorpio.

If their emotions get totally out-of-control then do use one of the Bach Flower Essences as described in Chapter Four.

My Scorpio says he/she never want to see/hear from me ever again.

This can be tricky if you're an Aquarius. Aquarius so loves to have friends, even ex-lovers that to hear all contact has been curtailed can feel like the ultimate rejection but you will have to respect the decision.

If you're a Pisces, read that sentence again and believe it. They don't want to see you again, which means you have caused them to feel so unhinged that seeing you again will push them over the edge, and you don't want to be accused of that do you?

They have told you the truth, at this moment in time, they don't want to see you or hear from you.

Period (as they say in the USA)

Full Stop (as we say in the UK)

Scorpio either is, or they're not. They either like you, or not and if it's love, they either love you, or they don't and if they don't love you, you're taking up space in their lives that they want to devote to the one they *do* love.

End of.

If you're a little older, you might recall the agony of Elizabeth Taylor and Richard Burton's love affair. She was a floppy Pisces, he was an intense Scorpio. He had an Aries Ascendant (assertive) and Moon in Virgo (worrisome) and she had a Sagittarius Ascendant (tell-it-like-it-is) and Moon in Scorpio (intense) and they were married and divorced twice but kept in contact.

Here is an excerpt from a letter Richard sent her after they were divorced for the second time:

"I love you, lovely woman. If anybody hurts you, just send me a line saying something like 'Need' or 'Necessary' or just the one magic word 'Elizabeth', and I will be there somewhat faster than sound."

Their romance was kept in the news as it started on the set of the film Cleopatra in 1963 that they were both starring in. It resulted in them having an affair, as they were both already married to other people but, of course, the motion picture company eventually loved the publicity.

All I can remember about it was a joke that went around one of the schools I went to, which was 'Elizabeth Taylor went for a Burton' from the British phrase: 'Gone for a Burton' meaning dead or finished.

Chapter Seven

The Solutions

Now that you have learned a little about Scorpio and how they think and feel, I'm now going to explain how to build trust with one.

Don't expect it to be easy or swift.

Let's go back to my trusty dictionary for a definition of what trust is:

Firm belief in reliability or truth or strength etc of a person or thing, state of being relied on, confident expectation, thing or person committed to one's care, resulting obligation.

To build up trust with your Scorpio first of all you're going to have to have a strong idea of who *you* are. A Scorpio will have spent the whole of their life (and maybe even preceding lives) knowing who they are, what they hate, where their soft spots are, what they do and don't like.

If you're not too sure who you are, or where you're going in your life, you're not going to be terribly appealing to our 8th sign.

Being indecisive is not something a Scorpio suffers from, so if you're a Gemini or Libra, get yourself into a firmer state of mind.

Unless it can be proved otherwise, your Scorpio only wants the best for you and everyone around them, so equally you will have to be firm in your convictions and tastes.

You will have to go slowly, Scorpio is not a swift sign energy. You will have to have a passion and that passion can be about anything, as long as you feel it deeply and truly. A shared passion is good, or even a complementary one will do. You might be into music, he/she might be into dance. The two things go well together. You might love a certain hobby or past time, maybe hill walking. As long as your interest and theirs combine in some way, things will go well.

Here's Jack, a young Scorpio man who works in a magazine publisher as a graphic artist. Here he is talking about a relationship he got into and what went on for him while it was happening:

> *I can get really, really jealous, and often I make a drama out of nothing but at the time I don't realise it because my feelings are very intense. She means everything to me, but my feelings can very easily shift to the opposite, and when it happens, that's where the stuff starts to get bad: I'm saying and doing things that I really shouldn't. I often felt betrayed (unreasonably), underestimated, and I came to feeling all of this because of...nothing. We could go out sometimes to a pub or something, and if I see her staring at some other guy, boom, my mood changed completely, I value her completely differently and then there's a drama scene at home. I simply CAN'T OVERCOME THIS, because at the time the only truth there is, is what I feel. It actually is like that all the time. I have only one truth and one guide — my feelings.*

Now compare this to someone on the receiving end of this type of behaviour. Here we have Patricia, a London-based Aquarius interior designer who has dated (but never married) a number of Scorpio men:

> *I went out with him when I was in Notting Hill. We had a brief relationship but stayed friends and occasional lovers for much longer. He was quite a character, he dressed in velvet jackets and vintage clothes and behaved like the Lord of the Manor. He was a stone restorer and was passionate about architecture and antiques. He lived in a big house he was doing up and this took him at least ten years. The end result was featured in a design magazine. He*

was also a bit mad and possibly an alcoholic. He had a bunch of pub friends who he met every day and his favourite pastime was to get very drunk and watch porn with his mates. He was definitely not the marrying sort. He had an extremely complicated love life and usually had about four or five women none of which knew about the other ones. I actually knew about all his other women and didn't really care but he was not a good person to have a relationship with!

He was too full of secrets and I think he enjoyed playing one woman off against the other. In the end he got together with an older woman, she was very posh and bossy. Unfortunately, she got cancer and he landed up looking after her. I saw him after she had died and it had really flattened him. He was quite depressed. I stayed friends with him for a long time but I found his boozy lifestyle ultimately boring. I last saw him about two years ago on a train station. He saw me and then walked up the other end of the platform. At first, I was hurt but that was typical of his behaviour. A lot of people hated him, especially women.

These are real people, that live in the same world as you and me, and it seems sad that they're not living their dream or being happy.

Problems occur in a Scorpio's world when their foundations are wobbly. Let's go back to Pluto for a moment. Remember how it's a distant planet, with an egg-shaped orbit. It doesn't 'do' stuff the same as the other planets. It's different. It's strange.

That's how a Scorpio can feel. That they're 'outside' of the ordinary world, that they're more in touch with that enormous world of feelings, that goes on and on and on, and will last forever. And in that type of living, they forget about the real physical world that exists…and they would feel happier if they touched-in every now and then.

I'm not suggesting that Scorpio loses their passion or their drive, but a little self-restraint every now and then will prevent them from tipping over into la la land.

If you or your Scorpio are having emotional problems, take a teeny step back for a minute and maybe use one of the flower essences I mentioned earlier or one of the suggestions below.

I've divided the Scorpios into the different Moon or Ascendants, as it's these that will differentiate and individualise your help.

Aries Asc or Moon

Stand Back! Don't get too close! An Aries/Scorpio that's upset will drive through walls to get to the truth. Help them with action, physical action. Do some Judo, Taekwondo, Fencing (watch you don't get stabbed by mistake!), Squash, anything that is physically demanding and needs lots of energy to play out all the emotion.

Taurus Asc or Moon

This combination will want physical needs met but in a much calmer and more sensitive way. Good food, good wine (not too much, you don't want to lose the plot!) good sex, good massage...anything where the bodies needs are totally met. To make them feel happier, make a nice meal or get them in the kitchen and bake some biscuits/cookies, they'll soon start to feel settled.

Gemini Asc or Moon

Get a good book. The bible will do (any version) quote some passages, quote some more, get a conversation going. If this still doesn't work, pop them in a car for a short journey (works every time) and let them pour their heart out while you drive. Motion and company help and I think also the fact that you're both facing the same way, as opposed to in conversation when you're generally face-to-face, which an upset Scorpio will not prefer.

Cancer Asc or Moon

Wear your sympathy hat and look concerned and empathic. Get your Cancer/Scorp to describe, in and all its emotional detail exactly how they feel. You can't escape the onslaught, so be prepared for strong emotions and heart-felt deep feelings to surface. Lean into their space and show you care. You don't have to say anything and listening carefully will help the most. You could also do some home cooking to lighten things as Cancer/Scorps love cooking.

Leo Asc or Moon

Do *not* ignore the Leo/Scorp. Tell them they have your undivided attention and ask 'How can I help, what can I DO?' They won't want sympathy, but they may want to rant and rave for a few minutes until they feel a little better. They will want a little sincere praise, a hint of red-carpet treatment and some acknowledgement for their suffering. In a few hours, they'll be back to their bright and breezy self, but ignore them at your peril.

Virgo Asc or Moon

Virgo/Scorps are wonderful at worrying. Then they will worry that they're worrying. This is Not a Good Thing. You will need some trusty Homeopathic Ignatia or the Bach Flower Essence Centaury and will need to take some time to unravel what's been going on. Best approach is a quiet lie-down so their brains can switch off for a while.

Libra Asc or Moon

Relationships and Love will concern Libra/Scorps. Gentle aromatherapy massage, pastel colours, everyone being 'nice' works best. As Libra is an Air sign and Scorpio a Water sign you might find a fog happening and not know how to help. Calm surroundings that are beautiful, exquisite flowers, Art in all its forms and politeness will also work well. Don't even think about arguing, as you'll end up with a further mess.

Scorpio Asc or Moon

Revenge and drastic actions will be on the mind of a double Scorp. Try and head them off by helping them do drastic stuff without it hurting anyone. Letter writing to the people concerned and then ritualistically burning the letter works well, as does creating lots of space between the antagonists and your Scorpio. Do NOT indulge in any of their fantasies, which might be considerable and reassure them that you ARE on their side but you're not going to get drawn-in. Be firm. Be strong. This is when you need to match their inner bravery with your support.

Sagittarius Asc or Moon

A philosophic debate about the pros and cons of whatever is happening will bring good rewards. Studying the problem in an intelligent, reasoned way helps a Sag/Scorp move forward. If you can quote one or another philosophers views on this, all the better. Arrangements made for a nice, long trip away to an exotic foreign country will also send them into nirvana.

Capricorn Asc or Moon

Be realistic, practical and offer sensible solutions. Get the family involved. Cap/Scorp wants the real worldview, not something wishy-washy or 'new age'. If a distant relative has suffered in a similar way, point this out and also point out how they recovered and suggest your Cap/Scorp might also do the same. Check out legal options and financial and make a written plan of 'what-to-do-next'.

Aquarius Asc or Moon

The wackier the solution the better. A day collecting seashells on the beach, a visit to a miners cottage, a trip up a craggy mountain dressed as a hermit, anything that involves ideas that aren't 'the norm'. Get outside as fresh air really helps this sign combination and you might find they soon calm down as they feel the breeze on their face, or the sun on their body. As Aquarius is such an altruistic sign, you could help out on the soup-run, or spend a day collecting cast-offs for a charity.

Pisces Asc or Moon

Now you will need what I call the fairy option. Pisces/Scop doesn't want a practical solution and will be worrying about their spiritual purpose and how their karma is doing. A few days in a retreat, a psychic reading or two, incense, candles, fairy/angel cards will all help...and lots of sleep. After a few night of dream sharing, they'll soon be back to normal.

Chapter Eight

Trusting Tactics

Got to trust someone
Trust someone
Someone you trust
Got to be careful
Be careful
From 'Bandit' by Neil Young

Now that you know a little more about how a birth chart works, you should have a good idea of what sort of Scorpio is in your life.

Are they an Airy Scorpio, wanting ideas and discussion, or a Firey Scorpio, running off to save-the-world or are they an Earthy Scorpio wanting meals on time and all the pleasures of the flesh, or a Watery Scorpio, tearful at times and very sensitive?

Whatever type they are, we now need to discuss the most important part of this book: what trusting is all about.

My dictionary defines trust as: *firm belief in the reliability or truth or strength etc. of a person or thing, state of being relied on; confident expectation, the thing or person committed to one's care, resulting obligation.*

Trust is a big word for a Scorpio. Without trust, their lives become angry, upset and dangerous. If we think a little first about the images of Pluto, such a small planet, so far, far away from the Earth, such a strange orbit and a surface that is cold as ice, we can get a better idea of what goes on with a Scorpio when they want to have that trust in their lives.

Let's ask three totally different Scorpios for their views:

Here's Sandy who works at a ski resort on a mountain in

British Columbia as a waitress:

"Trust is feeling safe with someone. Safe to show them who I am, to be myself and drop any guards. Trust is feeling unconditional love."

Here's Marie, a single mother who lives in Scotland with her three children and partner:

"Trust is when you feel so comfortable with something that you can give it your all, whether being a person or circumstance."

And Brian a finance manager of a large supply company in Paris:

"Trust — being able to depend on someone (family, friend or colleague) completely, knowing that they'll never let you down."

There are three themes that come out of these sentences: safe, comfortable and dependable. For your Scorpio to trust you they need to feel those three things.

So what is safe? Back the dictionary again.

Safe — free of danger or injury: affording security or not involving risks.

Comfortable — giving ease and contentment; feeling at ease or free from pain, trouble, or hardship

Depend — be controlled or determined, be unable to do without.

Luke is a Scorpio in his late thirties and works as a therapist with disadvantaged youth in a large inner city in the UK. He was abused as a kid. This is a serious trust issue and one he still struggles with:

I have feelings of extreme hate towards the people concerned. It may not come up often, but it does come up and usually as a reaction to me feeling the emotions around the situation, especially if mixed with frustration or feelings of being ineffective. Psychically I want to destroy them. Physically I make sure I'm not around them if at all vulnerable to the feelings of hate — it could turn nasty, and that's not helpful! Underlying these extreme feelings, which are hot blooded, are cold thoughts of 'one day I'll get my chance'. Maybe that will be in letting their friends or colleagues know the situation and their behaviour. Maybe it will be being able to watch their world fall apart.

Being self-aware, he knows that there is no easy way to resolve this:

Spiritually I'm not happy with any of this, and work at making peace with them and with myself. It all does get better with time but it will still arise, just less frequently rather than less intently. And it can all come falling down on me, with feelings of despair, ineffectiveness and a desire to disappear from existence. It will go wrong, I fail, I'm all alone, no one cares, I'm unable to make the fundamental change, feeling of being in a deep dark hole etc.

So to get your Scorpio to trust you, you will have to help them feel safe, comfortable and you must be dependable. So, it's no good saying one thing, and doing another. It's no good changing your mind (a terrible Libran trait) or in fact talking too much

A quick way to wear out a Scorpio is to have non-stop chatter going on. They're more likely to switch off completely and not listen. What they will be doing is going under the surface and checking how you're actually feeling, then saying something so astute, you get caught short.

It happens.

I know.

Your Scorpio Child

Your Scorpio child can challenge even the most docile of parents if they don't get a few important things sorted-out early on.

One of which is 'who is the parent?'

As your child will have been born as an 'old soul', they can easily think and act as if they know best about everything, which can be a little tiring.

And then there is the issue about intensity. How do you welcome that intensity and stop it taking over your life?

Here are some suggestions from Scorpios themselves about how they would like to be parented. So if you can get a few of these in place, while they are young, it will prevent a whole heap of problems while they're growing-up.

Here is Belinda Cancer Asc, Sun Scorpio in the 5th, Moon Pisces who has a Pisces mum and Cancer step-dad talking about her childhood:

I was extremely headstrong about clothes. I refused to wear any of the clothes my mother chose. At two years old, she recognized that the easiest way to deal with this was to take me shopping and ask what I liked. I shook my head yes or no for each item. Being given a choice, even at that incredibly young age, was a very smart move!

My parents let my blowups pass without trying to mollify me or convince me I was wrong to feel as I did.

No one ever entered my room without permission. When we argued, I was always given the chance to fully express how I felt. I was never told I was 'just a kid' or 'didn't know anything' or was 'too young to understand'. I was treated with the kind of respect they gave other adults. If I was too emotional to talk I was encouraged to write them a letter, of whatever length, to express how I felt.

My interests (keeping and breeding fish, collecting rocks, bringing random wildlife home to be 'rescued') were always supported, even when I started asking for books on herb lore, astrology, tarot and other potentially 'occult' topics.

I was shy as a kid and hated answering the phone, talking to cashiers, answering the door, or meeting total strangers. Neither of my parents ever forced me to do any of the above and allowed me to either slowly warm up to the idea/person or to choose not to interact with them.

Here is Daniella, another young Scorpio lady with Moon in Gemini explaining how she would like to be parented:

If the parents are honest, direct, firm, devoted, and affectionate. You could say all children need this but I suspect the Scorpio child in particular needs to see that their parents have integrity, in order for the child to respect them. Also, the parents need to be good listeners, which means both listening when the child has something to say that they may not want to hear (if the child is depressed or angry) without trying to fix it, but also equally means listening when the child says they aren't ready to talk. This is all part of building trust, a trust that might be innate for another child but for a Scorpio has to be regularly measured and verified. 'Will you respect your own and my boundaries? Will you say what you mean? Will you care enough to really listen to me?' Witnessing personal courage would also be a benefit, as it would guide the Scorpio to overcome their sensitivity and be proactive in life when needed.

Here is an Aquarius mother talking about her Scorpio daughter.

My daughter said that being honest with her was and still is very important to her. She wishes she hadn't got taken in by Disney movies 'happy-ever-after-ending' as reality is much tougher. We talked about the tantrums she had when she was little and how I learnt to just let her be when she had a tantrum, she quickly got over them that way. Also expect and accept the moods, don't demand smiles all day long. My daughter got fed up with a teacher that kept telling her to smile, so she refused to smile for him at all. Another teacher she refused to speak to at all as she didn't like him. They are not the best communicators when little but being honest with them and showing them that you are on their side no matter what, will have them opening up.

Here's Wendy, a Libran mum talking about when her son Charlie was a toddler:

Charlie also had a great daredevil side to his character but he would try to weigh up the situation first, decide it was doable and go for it — sometimes he had some awful injuries but never moaned and half the time I didn't even know he had been hurt till his brother told me or I saw him in his bath covered in cuts and bruises — very stoical to this day. Never makes a fuss but quite likes a bit of TLC if others notice his wounds but one has to be careful not to be too sorry for him because he is very proud and sees it as weakness. I do wonder if a lot of his later daring dos were simply proving to his brother he could do it as some of the things he did were far too much for his age — making rope swings across a lake in the field next to our garden when he was barely out of nursery etc! He had the brain for it but not the muscle strength or height to succeed.

I used to take lots of photos and many of them have Charlie sticking his tongue out when photographed in family pics — the camera would catch a twinkle in his eye then a quick tongue out or pulling a funny face but if anyone looked at him he would revert to being angelic. He wanted to be a bit naughty but hated being told off and would take it very hard, hiding in his room painting his War Hammer figures for hours.

This made me chuckle as it was almost identical to what Belinda pointed out from her childhood:

My mother still talks about a commercial that aired when I was tiny that she felt was totally apt for my temper. In it, a little girl is playing quietly and sweetly with her toys until her brother walks over to take one. She lets him take it but as soon as he turns his back, the little girl morphs into a gigantic beastly monster, eats him in one gulp, and regains her toy. She smiles, transforms back into an angelic form, and goes back to sweetly playing by herself. My parents likewise let my blowups pass without trying to mollify me or convince me I was wrong to feel as I did.

So top of the list then is find a way to vent their anger and other powerful feelings…and not to stress when that is happening.

Your Scorpio Boss

Trust is the glue of life. It's the most essential ingredient in effective communication. It's the foundational principle that holds all relationships.
Stephen Covey Author of *The 7 Habits of Highly Effective People*
(Sun Scorpio, Moon Leo)

What I consider to be amazing about the above quote is the title of the book that his son Stephen M R Covey wrote called 'The Speed of Trust'. I have no idea (and no way of knowing) what star sign Covey junior is, but we know for sure that his dad Covey senior is a Scorpio. So he must have instilled (rather deeply if you ask me) in his son the most important thing in his life as a businessperson: 'Trust'.

So what's it like to have a Scorpio boss? What's it like to work for someone who is Scorpio?

As we know, you need to be deeply focused to mirror a Scorpio, so working for them will produce the same needs. You must also be totally honest. There is no way you will be able to pull the wool over their eyes, or pretend things are fine, when they're not. You'll also have to be strong and steady. Fluffy won't work here.

If you want to impress your Scorpio boss, don't tell him too much about yourself. Become an enigma. Leave stuff back. Keep yourself to yourself and only open up when asked.

He/She will want you to do the work, not bring your personal life into the workplace. You will be expected to turn up on time, do your job, be focused on results and never, never let the side down.

I know more self-employed Scorpios than employed. They seem to enjoy the challenge of creating their own little world or business and they are generally very good at what they do. Their focused, fixed attention can bring them the results they have aimed at.

And don't think that these attributes are exclusively male. Both Hillary Clinton Secretary of State in the USA and Condoleezza Rice who preceded her are Scorpios and I'm sure there are quite a few people employed in their teams who respect their ability to do their work and not get side-tracked by frivolity.

Your (male) Scorpio Lover

To successfully date a Scorpio male you need to be strong in personality and ideas. Flaky won't work. You will also need to be devoted to him.

This will sound hard for the more flighty signs or for people not that interested in commitment. If you want a fling, you'll have one. I've got lots of stories in my files of clients who have had brief affairs with Scorpios, some producing children, some not but they didn't manage to make a long-term relationship.

I also know a lot of good Scorpio/Capricorn relationships as Capricorn is so steady and forward focused, they don't worry about a Scorpio being all emotional.

You might also find that you're not the only person who is interested in your Scorpio man, a lot of other women might be too, so getting one to settle down can be a challenge.

As Jimmy Savile, Sun Scorpio, Moon Virgo the DJ said in his autobiography:

"...there have been trains and, with apologies to the hit parade, boats and planes (I am a member of the 40,000 ft club) and bushes and fields, corridors, doorways, floors, chairs, slag heaps, desks and probably everything except the celebrated chandelier and ironing board." [9]

Jimmy never married and died single.

In our example chart Cheiro, who had Sag Asc and Moon in Virgo was also a confirmed bachelor until his health took a turn for the worse and a lady he had met nursed him back to wellness:

I had a long, hard fight for life; she nursed me night and day... We took a voyage to make my recovery complete. One day on the return journey to England I had a good look at the lines of my hand. I saw I was approaching the date when marriage was marked for me late in life. I went down to the writing room and wrote my resignation to the Anti-marriage Society, to which I had belonged to for more than thirty years. For fear I might weaken in my resolution, I gave the letter to my future wife to post and we were married on my return home. [10]

What made him change his mind was something dramatic and life threatening. Now I'm not suggesting that you make your Scorpio ill, then nurse him back to health but if you can 'be' with him while he's going through something difficult or challenging and remain cool, calm and collected, you'll have him bending down on one knee, ring in hand.

Your (female) Scorpio Lover

To successfully date a Scorpio woman, you will need to know

that actions speak much louder than words.

Here is Jennifer (who is also a Scorpio) talking about her new Scorpio man. What was interesting was her not even wanting to see him touching fingers with another woman, let alone kissing or being near to her:

I was standing in front of them and he, again, put his hand on her chair rest and she positioned her arm and hand next to his and they sort of interlocked pinky and index fingers, either in a friendly awkward way or something more. I, of course, felt my skin crawl and got so nervous that I went quiet and rigid. He knew something was wrong and started to really give me a lot of attention from that point on. I took some of the attention, but decided to give him a little bit of a chilly shoulder as a way to protect myself. I said nothing was wrong when he asked me, but I really wanted to leave right then and there.

It wasn't sufficient that he told her 'hundreds of times a day' that he loved her. It wasn't enough for him to have talked of 'marriage and babies'. When she saw him touching some other woman she felt her 'skin crawl'.

Now, you could say she's overreacting, which she might be, but the underlying message is, she wants to trust him emotionally, spiritually, physically AND visibly.

I know quite a number of successful Scorpio/Scorpio relationships, as they both understand the trust issue and this one eventually settled down when she wrote him a letter.

Sometimes putting thoughts and feelings onto paper is better than talking.

What to do when your Scorpio relationship has ended

One thing is for sure, a Scorpio relationship that's destined to end, won't end quietly or smoothly. If you're a Fire sign, you will have masses of arguments before it ends. If you're Earth, things will jog along getting worse and worse until someone pulls the plug. If you're an Air sign, you just won't understand what went wrong and will feel terribly perplexed and if you're a Water sign, you'll slowly edge away from each other, getting more and more confused, anxious, and bogged down with all the emotions swirling around.

Here are a few trusty and tried tips to help you feel better.

Fire Sign

If you're a Fire sign: Aries, Leo or Sagittarius and you are now in the aftermath of the relationship my best advice is to use the Element you're ruled by, which is fire. Now I'm not suggesting that you tear up all their clothes and make a bonfire in the garden, or set alight to their favourite books. No, we're going to do something much more empowering.

Get a candle, any type will do but the best would be a small nightlight and light it and recite:

"I......(your name) do let you......(Scorpio's name) go, in freedom and with love so that I am free to attract my true soul-love."

Leave the candle in a safe place to burn down. At least an hour's worth of burn time is good. Be careful not to leave the house and keep an eye on it.

Then over the next few days, gather up any belongings that are your (now) ex-Scorpio's and either deliver them to your ex's house, or give them to a charity.

If you have any photos, don't be in a big rush to tear them all up, as some Fire signs are prone to as you might regret this years later. When you have the strength, keep a few of the nicer photos, and discard the rest.

Earth Sign

If you are an Earth sign: Taurus, Virgo or Capricorn you will feel less inclined to do something drastic or outrageous (unless of course you have a Fire sign Moon...).

The end of your relationship should involve the Element of Earth and this is best tackled using some trusty crystals.

The best ones to use are the ones associated with your Sun sign and also with protection. The following crystals are considered protective but are also birthstones from *Cunningham's Encyclopedia of Crystal, Gem and Metal Magic*, by Scott Cunningham.

Taurus = Emerald
Virgo = Agate
Capricorn = Onyx

Take your Crystal and cleanse it in fresh running water. Wrap it in some tissue paper then take yourself on a long walk into the country. When you find a suitable spot, dig a small hole and place the crystal in the ground.

Think about how your relationship has ended. Remember the good times and the bad. Forgive yourself for any mistakes you think you may have made. Then imagine a beautiful plant growing where you have buried the crystal and the plant blossoming and growing strong. This represents your new love that will be with you when the time is right.

Air Sign

If you are an Air sign: Gemini, Libra or Aquarius you might want to talk about what happened first before you feel happy enough to end your connection. Air signs need reasons and answers and can waste precious life-energy looking for those answers.

Here's Natalie, a young Gemini lady talking about how she felt after her early Scorpio relationship ended:

I met him a few years later, was terrified to go, had no idea how would I feel. But it felt empty, I have no feelings left for him, nothing. But I always need to UNDERSTAND things. And this unfinished business keeps replaying in my head once in a while and probably will be for the rest of my life because I need to UNDER-STAND what happened, how and why and I never will, because he didn't tell me and surely won't tell me now. I could probably get back together with him if I wanted to. But I don't, I just need to get my questions answered.

Forgive yourself first of all for the relationship ending. It's no one's fault and time will heal the wounds. When you are having a better day and your thoughts are clear, get a piece of paper and write your (ex) Scorpio a letter.

This isn't a letter you are actually going to post, so you can be as honest as you want with your thoughts.

Write to them thus:

"Dear Mr/Ms/Miss Scorpio,
I know you will be happy now that you're in your new life but there are a few things I want you to know and understand that you overlooked when we were together."

Then list all the annoying habits, comments (Air signs seem to remember people's words more than any other Element) who-was-right and what-went-wrong.

Top of the list might be their inability to explain to you how they were feeling and what was going through their mind.

Make sure you write every little detail, down to how they seemed to disagree with everything you said.

Keep writing until you can write no more. Then end your letter with something positive and empowering, as you want to keep your karma as intact as possible.

Maybe something along the lines of:

"Even though we went through hell together and never saw eye to eye, I wish you well on your path."

Then take the letter somewhere windy and high, out of town maybe where you won't be disturbed. Maybe the top of a hill overlooking a beautiful view, on a pier during a blustery day or maybe on a cliff face, but do be sensible and don't put yourself in any personal danger.

Read through your letter again. Make sure it sounds right in your head then ceremoniously tear a small part of your letter into the smallest pieces possible and let those small pieces of paper be whisked away by the wind.

I don't think I good idea to dispose of *your entire* letter in this way, because a) it might be rather long and you'd be guilty of littering and b) you also run the risk of it blowing somewhere inconvenient so save the rest of it. When you get home, burn the rest of the letter safely in an ashtray and pop it in the rubbish or put it in the paper shredder and add to your paper recycling.

Water Sign

If you are a Water sign: Cancer, Scorpio or Pisces it might be a little harder for you to recover from your broken heart. Not impossible but you might lie awake at night wondering if you've done the right thing by finishing the relationship, or feeling deeply hurt that the relationship has ended. Don't fret. Things will get better but you need to be able to get through those first difficult weeks without bursting into tears all the time.

Your emotional healing needs to involve the water element. So here is a well-used suggestion. This is a powerful way to heal the emotional hurt and it allows you to use that part of you that is most 'in tune' with the issue.

It involves your tears.

The next time you feel weepy, collect your tears into a glass. This isn't as hard as it sounds. There you are, tears falling at a rapid rate, threatening to flood the world, all you need is *one* of those tears to fall into a glass of water. I recommend using a nice glass. Something pretty that has some meaning for you.

Ensure the tear has fallen in, then top-up with enough water almost to the rim of the glass.

Place the glass on a table, maybe with a lit candle, maybe with a photo of you together, whatever feels right for you, and then recite the following:

This loving relationship with you:.......has ended.
I reach out across time and space to tell you that our love has ended.
My tears will wash away the hurt I feel.
I release you from my heart, mind and soul.
We part in peace.

Then slowly drink the water.

Spend the next few weeks talking about how you feel to someone who truly cares.

Your Scorpio Friend

I owe much to my friends; but, all things considered, it strikes me that I owe even more to my enemies. The real person springs life under a sting even better than under a caress.
Andre Gide
(Sun Scorpio in 2nd, Moon Cancer)

As I mentioned earlier, Scorpios quite a lot of the time, make friends with other Scorpios. Already the trust issue is resolved and there is a sense of affinity and being able to see the world in the same way.

I have had a number of Scorpio friendships over the years. Some were better than others. One thing I learned was there is no need to be 'in contact' all the time. Your Scorpio friendship will be the same as you left it, regardless of what you might have been doing in the meantime.

Layla is in her late forties and works for a large international haulage company in their head office in Europe and has Libra Ascendant, Scorpio Sun in the First and Moon in Scorpio.

She is multilingual having studied Spanish and French at University.

I asked her how long she kept friendships for and here is her reply:

With close friends, it can be a very long time — I still keep in (spasmodic) touch with a girl I met on my very first day at school at age 4 and half. I've known one of my closest friends since we were 10. We don't live in the same country now and keep in touch by phone and email with occasional meetings. When we do meet, it's as if we'd seen each other the day before. Same thing with a very dear friend in Liverpool whom I met when we were both overseas on university placement — we didn't even go to the same university (she was at Liverpool and I went to Newcastle) so we saw each other after our university courses had finished and I was able to afford a car. Ditto an ex-work colleague in the US (who is also a Scorpio) — not much day-to-day contact, just occasional meetings which never have any awkward silences, despite the distance and cultural differences — or maybe because of them.

To make friends with a Scorpio, all the previous rules apply: be honest, be trusting, keep personal information safe but also there is no need to be with them all the time. Scorpios can be quite independent and self-sufficient and they won't need to be in your pocket all the time. They will be there for you if life gets tricky, or your life implodes and equally they will expect you to be there for them if things get drastic.

Your Scorpio Mum

As with everything in Astrology, getting on with someone better helps if you take into account your own sign, not just the sign of the person you are trying to understand. So if you want to get on better with your Scorpio mother, you will have to think about the sign that you are. It also helps if you check your own chart and look for points of connection. Are your Moons in the same sign? Are your Ascendants the same or of the same Element?

If your mother is a Scorpio and you're a Water sign, she will seem like a true goddess to you and be able to empathise with your every feeling. If you're a Fire sign there might be lots of conflict as you will be speeding around, expecting her to catch up with you, when she's barely started...the hare and the tortoise comes to mind.

I know so many wonderful Scorpio mothers. They are intent on ensuring their offspring are safe and secure and away from anything that might hurt them. They equally will not want to hurt their children too much...unless there are some terrible incompatibilities.

Here's a Scorpio mum talking about her Scorpio son:

...through trying to raise my son I'm recognizing many things that I don't agree with how my mother raised me. Being honest, firm but kind and allowing the time and space for change(s) *to be* processed *is important. I never dealt well with my emotions as a child, and bottled everything up, until situations became volcanic. I was never taught how to acknowledge my feelings and find a positive way of expressing them.*

Your Scorpio mum will find change difficult and will need some time for things to 'sink in'. Also remember it's no good expecting them not to be emotional about things but you don't have to enter in to those emotions. Wait for them to pass.

I have a Scorpio auntie (I love aunties, they're great!) but as she lives on the other side of the world to me, I don't see her much. In fact, I've only met her once. But I do know one of her sons (my cousin) is a Pisces and I've never heard through the family grapevine him complain about her. Why should he? They're both Water signs.

Equally, I have a Scorpio cousin on the other side of my family and I know he loves and was loved by his mum my other auntie and what helped him the most was his Sagittarius Ascendant as she was a Gemini.

No, your Scorpio mother will be loyal to you and goodness help anyone who tries to tell you otherwise.

They might not run the school committee or invite everyone round for tea all the time but they will want the best for you, every mother does. What you need to remember though is they're quite capable of direct honesty, so if you don't like something, tell them.

I have worked a lot with Scorpio mothers over the years and I admire their sticking power and their ability to stay focused on their children.

Your Scorpio Dad

A Scorpio father is a strong presence in any family. Determined, focused and deeply aware of people's feelings. I don't totally agree with Linda Goodman that they will fix you with a hypnotic stare. I know plenty of Scorpios that will barely make eye contact. Keep in mind the Elements.

Is your dad an airy Scorpio, wanting to chat about this and that and good at telling you stories and having conversational sparring matches?

Or is he an Earthy Scorpio, concerned with how you're going to earn a living and helping you financially, and maybe even welcoming you into the family business?

Or is your father a Firey Scorpio, dashing off to work and round the world. Here one day, gone the next. Sporty and full of energy and enthusiasm?

Or maybe your male parent is a Watery one, with tears in his eyes when he tells you how worried he is about you, and wanting hugs and tactile contact?

See how your dad's Elements fits with yours and work out how they match, or get a good astrologer to help you. What you will need to know is how you blend together and what your own expectations of being parented are. As with Scorpio mum they're quite OK with being told 'the truth' so don't hold back with your thoughts and feelings and equally don't expect him to agree or react. He'll file it away somewhere as a fact unless you tell him otherwise.

Your Scorpio Sibling

If you have a Scorpio sibling, one thing you must learn very early on, is not to enter their room or personal space without permission. You must also never read their journal or diary and you must learn to give them space to just 'be'.

If you have to share rooms, make sure there is a clear division of space and your side is yours, and theirs is their own.

You will come across grumpiness and moodiness. I lived with my Scorpio friend for a while and she was terrible first thing in the morning. It took her quite a while to come round and be capable of communication. She wanted peace and quiet, which hardly ever happens in a domestic set-up especially if there are lots of kiddies around. The only way to deal with that, if it bothers you, is to just let it happen. You can't change them, so don't try. Just get on and do other things.

My brother-in-law is Scorpio and I asked my lovely husband what it was like growing up with an older Scorpio brother. He told me that it was no good arguing, no good disagreeing or telling him he was wrong about anything. While they were growing up the 60s was in full swing and his brother loved the whole new world that had been created with Bob Dylan and being a hippie...that didn't go down well with conservative parents born in the 1920s and as much as his brother rebelled against 'the system' his parents viewed it as rebelling against them, and a whole passage of misunderstandings started. They never fell out though and are still very firmly 'related' to this day. They don't need to speak all the time but know how to contact each other if problems arise.

Try not to waste your precious life energy arguing with or disagreeing with your Scorpio sibling as all will happen is you'll feel exhausted, and they won't have changed a bit.

I hope you have enjoyed learning a little about the Sun Sign Scorpio. I hope you have managed to make a Birth Chart and understand it, and I hope you now know more about yourself and the Scorpio in your life.

If you would like to get in touch, please visit my website www.maryenglish.com

I wish you all the peace in the world, and happiness too.

References

1. *The Astrologers and Their Creed*, 1971, Christopher McIntosh, Arrow Books Ltd, 3 Fitzroy Square, London W1
2. http://news.bbc.co.uk/1/hi/4596246.stm
3. http://www.nasa.gov/audience/forstudents/k-4/stories/what-is-pluto-k4.html
4. Redefining the Solar System by Jenni Harte, http://www.astrologicalassociation.com/transit/sep2006/pluto.htm
5. http://bjork.com/#/past/discography/homogenic/track2/lyrics2
6. http://www.astrologysoftware.com/community/interviews/get_interview.asp?person_show=12
7. http://www.bristol.ac.uk/nsqi-centre/research/birch/index.html
8. The *Sunday Times* November 15, 2009
9. p139 *As it Happens*, Jimmy Savile OBE, His Autobiography, Jimmy Savile,1974, Barrie & Jenkins Lmited, London N3 1RX
10. *Confessions, Memoirs of a Modern Seer*, William Brendon and Sons Ltd, 1932 Count Lois Hammond, (Cheiro)

Bibliography

11 planets, A New View of the Solar System, David A Aguilar, 2008, National Geographic Society, Washington DC, USA

Essentials Astronomy, A Beginner's Guide to the Sky at Night, Paul Sutherland, 2007, Igloo Books Ltd, Sywell, NN6 0BJ, YK

Healing Pluto Problems, Donna Cunningham, 1986, Samuel Weiser Inc, York Beach, Maine USA

The Modern Text Book of Astrology (Revised Edition) Margaret E. Hone, 1980. L N Fowler & Co. Ltd, 1201/3 High Road, Chadwell Health, Romford, Essex, RM6 4DH

The Gods of Change, Pain, Crisis and the Transits of Uranus, Neptune and Pluto, Howard Sasportas, 1989, Arkana, Penguin Group, London W8 5TZ

Astrology and the Modern Psyche, Dane Rudyar, 1976, CRCS Publications, Vancouver, Washington, 98662

Pluto: The Evolutionary Journey of the Soul, Volume 1, Jeff Green, 1985, First Edition Fourteenth Printing, 2000, Llewellyn Publications, St Paul, MN, USA

Alive and Well with Pluto, Transits of Power and Renewal, Bil Tierney, 1999,Llewellyn Publications, St Paul, MN, USA

The Instant Astrologer, Felix Lyle and Bryan Aspland, 1998, Judy Piatkus Ltd, London W1P 1HF

Cunningham's Encyclopedia of Crystal, Gem and Metal Magic, by Scott Cunningham, published 1998, Llewellyn Publications, USA

Further Information

The Astrological Association
www.astrologicalassociation.com

The Bach Centre, The Dr Edward Bach Centre, Mount Vernon, Bakers Lane, Brightwell-cum-Sotwell, Oxon, OX10 0PZ, UK
www.bachcentre.com

Chart information and birth data from astro-databank at www.astro.com and www.astrotheme.com

ASCENDANT

Bo Derek, 20th November 1956, Long Beach CA, USA, 2.13pm, Aries Ascendant, Sun 8th, Moon in Cancer

Richard Burton, 10th November 1925, Pontrhydyfen Wales, 3pm, Aries Ascendant, Sun 8th, Moon in Virgo

Charles Manson, 12th November 1934, Cincinnati Ohio, USA, 4.40pm, Taurus Ascendant, Sun 7th, Moon Aquarius

Vivien Leigh, 5th November 1913, Darjeeling, India, 5.16pm, Taurus Ascendant, Sun 6th, Moon in Aquarius

Teddy, Theodore Roosevelt, 27th October 1858, New York, NY, USA, 7.45pm, Gemini Ascendant, Sun 5th, Moon in Cancer

Dorothy Day, 8th November 1897, Brooklyn, NY, USA, 6.50pm, Gemini Ascendant, Sun 5th, Moon in Taurus

Bill Gates, 28th October 1955, Seattle, WA, USA, 10pm, Cancer Ascendant, Sun 4th, Moon in Aries

Art Garfunkel, 5th November 1941, New York, NY, USA, 11pm, Leo Ascendant, Sun 3rd, Moon in Gemini

Lulu, 3rd November 1948, Lennoxtown, Scotland, 1.30am, Virgo Ascendant, Sun 3rd, Moon in Sagittarius

John Cleese, 27th October 1939, Weston-Super-Mare, 3.15am, Virgo Ascendant, Sun 2nd, Moon in Aries

Leonardo Dicaprio, 11th November 1974, Los Angeles, CA, USA, Libra Ascendant, Sun 2nd, Moon in Libra

Cleo Laine, 28th October 1927, Southall, England, 4.05am, Libra Ascendant, Sun 1st, Moon in Sagittarius

Tatum O'Neal, 5th November 1963, Los Angeles, CA, USA, 3.38am, Libra Ascendant, Sun 2nd, Moon in Cancer

Andre Gide, 22nd November 1869, Paris, France, 3am, Libra Ascendant, Sun 2nd, Moon in Cancer

Grace Kelly, Princess of Monaco, 12th November 1929, Philadelphia PA, USA, 5.31am, Scorpio Ascendant, Sun 1st, Moon Pisces

Jodie Foster, 19th November 1962, Los Angeles, CA, USA, 8.14am, Sagittarius Ascendant, Sun 12th, Moon in Virgo

Cheiro,1st November 1886, Dublin Ireland, 10.53am, Sagittarius Ascendant, Sun 11th, Moon in Virgo

King of England, Edward VII, 9th November 1841, 10.48am, London, Sagittarius Ascendant, Sun 11th, Moon in Virgo

Billie Jean King, Long Beach CA, USA, 22nd November 1943, 11.45am, Capricorn Ascendant, Sun 11th, Moon in Libra

Charles Bronson, 3rd November 1921, Croyle PA, USA, 11am, Capricorn Ascendant, Sun 11th, Moon in Sagittarius

Robert Louis Stevenson, 13th November 1880, Edinburgh, Scotland, 1.30pm, Aquarius Ascendant, Sun 10th, Moon in Pisces

Sylvia Plath, 27th October 1932, Boston MA, USA, 2.10pm, Aquarius Ascendant, Sun 9th, Moon in Libra

Whoopi Goldberg, 13th November 1955, New York, NY, USA, 12.49pm, Aquarius Ascendant, Sun 8th, Moon in Scorpio

Demi Moore, 11th November 1962, Roswell NM, USA, 2.16pm, Pisces Ascendant, Sun 8th, Moon in Taurus

Moon

Meg Ryan, 19th November 1961, Fairfield CT, USA, 10.36am, Capricorn Ascendant, Sun 11th, Moon in Aries

Bil Tierney, 4th November 1949, New York NY, USA, 4.41pm, Taurus Ascendant, Sun 7th, Moon in Taurus

Prince of Wales, Charles, 14th November 1948, London, 9.14pm, Leo Ascendant, Sun 4th, Moon in Taurus

Goldie Hawn, 21st November 1945, Washington DC, USA, 9.20am, Sagittarius Ascendant, Sun 12th, Moon in Gemini

Claude Monet, 14th November 1840, Paris, France, Moon in Cancer

Julia Roberts, 28th October 1967, Atlanta GA, USA, 12.16am, Cancer Ascendant, Sun 4th, Moon in Leo

Stephen Covey, 24th October 1932, Salt Lake City, Utah (no birth time), USA, Moon in Leo

Sean Combs, (Puff Daddy), 4th November 1969, Harlem New York, USA, Moon Virgo

Jimmy Savile OBE, 31st October 1936, Leeds, UK (no birth time) Moon Virgo

Bjork, 21st November 1965, Reykjavik Iceland, 7.50am, Scorpio Ascendant, Sun 1st, Moon in Scorpio

Michel Gauquelin, 13th November 1928, Paris, France, 10.15pm, Leo Ascendant, Sun 4th, Moon in Sagittarius

Ming-Na, 20th November 1963, Coloane Island Macau, Sun Scorpio, Moon Capricorn

William Herschel, 15th November 1738, Hanover, Germany, Sun Scorpio, Moon Capricorn

Francois Voltaire, 21st November 1694, Paris, France, 5.30pm, Gemini Ascendant, Sun 6th, Moon in Aquarius

Arthur M Young, 3rd November 1905, Paris France, 10.23am, Sagittarius Ascendant, Sun 11th, Moon in Aquarius

Neil Young, 12th November 1945, Toronto Ontario, Canada, Moon Aquarius

House

Sri Sathya Sai Baba, 23rd November 1926, Puttaparthy, India, 6.22am, Sagittarius Ascendant, Sun 1st, Moon in Cancer

Peter Cook, 17th November 1937, Torquay, England, 4.40am, Libra Ascendant, Sun 2nd, Moon in Taurus

k.d. lang, 2nd November 1961, Edmonton, Canada, 2.03am, Virgo Ascendant, Sun 2nd, Moon in Virgo

Picasso, 25th October 1881, Malaga, Spain, 11.15pm, Leo Ascendant, Sun 3rd, Moon in Sagittarius

Joni Mitchell, 7th November 1943, 10pm, Cancer Ascendant, Sun 4th, Moon in Pisces

Indira Ghandi, 19th November 1917, Allahabad, India, 11.11pm, Leo Ascendant, Sun in 4th , Moon in Capricorn

Marie-Antoinette Queen Consort, 2nd November 1755, Vienna,

Austria, 7.30pm, Cancer Ascendant, Sun 5th, Moon in Libra

Michael Dukakis, 3rd November 1933, Boston MA, 5.50pm, Gemini Ascendant, Sun 6th, Moon Taurus

Helen Reddy, 25th October 1941, Melbourne, Australia, 5.50pm, Aries Ascendant, Sun 7th, Moon in Capricorn

Griff Rhys-Jones, 16th November 1963, Cardiff, Wales, 3pm, Aries Ascendant, Sun 8th, Moon in Pisces

Tina Brown, 21st November 1953, Maidenhead, England, 1.30pm, Pisces Ascendant, Sun 9th, Moon in Gemini

Condoleezza Rice, Birmingham, AL, USA, Aquarius Ascendant, Sun 10th, Moon in Cancer

Winona Ryder, 29th October 1971, Rochester MN, USA, 11am, Sagittarius Ascendant, Sun 11th, Moon in Pisces

Hillary Clinton, 26th October 1947, Chicago, IL, USA, 8.02am, Scorpio Ascendant, Sun in 12th, Moon Pisces

Dodona Books offers a broad spectrum of divination systems to suit all, including Astrology, Tarot, Runes, Ogham, Palmistry, Dream Interpretation, Scrying, Dowsing, I Ching, Numerology, Angels and Faeries, Tasseomancy and Introspection.